HEALTHY MIND

A PRACTICAL GUIDE TO EMOTIONAL WELLNESS

DAVID SANDUA

ÍNDEX

I. INTRODUCTION TO EMOTIONAL WELLNESS

Emotional wellness is a crucial component of overall well-being, encompassing the ability to understand and manage our emotions effectively. It plays a significant role in how we navigate challenges, build relationships, and make decisions in our daily lives. In today's fast-paced and stressful world, it is essential to prioritize emotional wellness to maintain mental health and resilience. This introductory chapter will set the stage for exploring practical strategies to enhance emotional well-being. By delving into the foundations of emotional wellness, we can gain insights into the importance of self-awareness, self-regulation, and healthy coping mechanisms. Through a comprehensive understanding of emotional wellness, individuals can cultivate a greater sense of emotional balance and fulfillment in their lives. This chapter will lay the groundwork for the subsequent chapters, which will provide actionable steps and tools to promote a healthy mind and emotional resilience.

DEFINITION OF EMOTIONAL WELLNESS

Emotional wellness can be defined as the ability to navigate and cope with the full range of human emotions in a constructive and healthy manner. This includes the capacity to recognize, understand, and manage one's own emotions, as well as the ability to empathize with the emotions of others. Emotional wellness encompasses not just the absence of negative emotions such as anxiety or depression, but also the presence of positive emotions such as joy, gratitude, and contentment. It involves developing resilience in the face of adversity, maintaining healthy relationships, and engaging in self-care practices that promote emotional well-being. Cultivating emotional wellness requires a commitment to self-reflection, self-awareness, and ongoing personal growth. By prioritizing emotional wellness in our lives, we can enhance our overall mental health and quality of life.

IMPORTANCE OF A HEALTHY MIND IN OVERALL WELL-BEING

A healthy mind plays a crucial role in overall well-being, encompassing emotional, psychological, and mental facets. The beginning of this discussion revolves around the understanding that a healthy mind is the foundation upon which all other dimensions of wellness rest. It serves as a reservoir of resilience and coping strategies, enabling individuals to navigate life's challenges with clarity and adaptability. Moving to the middle section, the emphasis shifts to the interconnected nature of mental and physical health, underscoring how a sound mind contributes to physical well-being and vice versa. Additionally, a healthy mind fosters positive relationships, enhances productivity, and promotes a sense of purpose and fulfillment in life. In conclusion, prioritizing mental health is not merely a luxury but a necessity for holistic well-being, highlighting the indispensable role of emotional wellness in achieving a fulfilling and balanced life.

OVERVIEW OF THE GUIDE'S STRUCTURE AND OBJECTIVES

The guide 'Healthy Mind: A Practical Guide to Emotional Wellness' is structured in a comprehensive manner to provide readers with a detailed roadmap to improving their emotional well-being. The objectives of the guide are clearly outlined in each chapter, starting with an introduction to the importance of emotional wellness and its impact on overall health. Following this, chapters delve into specific strategies and techniques for managing stress, building resilience, and cultivating positive relationships. Each chapter builds upon the previous one, offering practical advice and exercises to help readers implement changes in their daily lives. The guide's structure ensures that readers progress from understanding the fundamental concepts of emotional wellness to actively engaging in behaviors that promote mental and emotional health. By organizing the guide in this way, readers are equipped with a step-by-step approach to enhancing their well-being and leading a more fulfilling life.

II. HISTORICAL PERSPECTIVES ON EMOTIONAL HEALTH

Historical perspectives on emotional health provide valuable insight into the evolution of how mental well-being has been perceived and addressed over time. From ancient civilizations such as the Greeks who believed in the connection between the mind and body, to the Middle Ages where mental health was often stigmatized and associated with witchcraft, to the modern era with the rise of psychology and psychotherapy, each period has shaped our understanding of emotions and mental health. By examining how different cultures and time periods have approached emotional wellness, we can gain a deeper understanding of the complexities surrounding mental health. Through analyzing the historical context of emotional health, we can appreciate the progress made in combating stigma and improving treatment options, while also recognizing the ongoing challenges and disparities that persist in today's society. Ultimately, historical perspectives serve as a crucial foundation for advancing our knowledge and promoting holistic well-being in the field of emotional health.

ANCIENT PHILOSOPHIES ON EMOTIONAL WELL-BEING

Ancient philosophies have long recognized the importance of emotional well-being in achieving a harmonious and fulfilling life. From the Stoics emphasizing the power of reason and self-control to the teachings of Buddhism on the impermanence of emotions, these ancient wisdom traditions offer valuable insights into managing our emotions. The Stoics believed that by practicing virtue and cultivating inner strength, one could achieve tranquility even in the face of adversity. Similarly, Buddhism teaches acceptance and mindfulness as tools for managing the ever-changing nature of emotions. By incorporating these age-old philosophies into modern approaches to emotional wellness, we can learn to navigate our emotions with greater clarity and resilience. Drawing on the timeless wisdom of these ancient traditions, we can cultivate a healthy mind that is more equipped to handle the challenges of everyday life.

EVOLUTION OF PSYCHOLOGICAL UNDERSTANDING OF EMOTIONS

The evolution of psychological understanding of emotions has been a dynamic and multifaceted journey that has shaped our current comprehension of how emotions function within the human mind. Early theories, such as the James-Lange theory, suggested that emotions are a physiological response to external stimuli, leading to the belief that emotions are simply reactions to specific events. However, as research and studies in the field of psychology have progressed, more nuanced perspectives have emerged. From the cognitive appraisal theory to the neurobiological perspective, modern psychology recognizes the complex interplay between cognition, physiology, and social factors in the experience and regulation of emotions. This evolution highlights the shifting landscape of emotional research, emphasizing the need for a holistic understanding that integrates various dimensions of human experience. As we continue to delve deeper into the intricacies of emotional wellness, this evolving understanding allows for more effective interventions and support for individuals seeking to cultivate a healthy mind.

IMPACT OF HISTORICAL VIEWS ON MODERN WELLNESS PRACTICES

The impact of historical views on modern wellness practices is crucial to understand in the pursuit of emotional wellness. Ancient philosophies such as those from Greece, Rome, and Asia have laid the foundation for many aspects of modern wellness practices. The mind-body connection emphasized by ancient Greeks like Hippocrates has been integrated into contemporary holistic approaches to health. Similarly, Chinese traditions such as acupuncture and Tai Chi have gained popularity in Western cultures for their therapeutic benefits. The historical perception of emotional well-being as interconnected with physical health has shaped the development of practices like mindfulness, meditation, and yoga in addressing modern mental health concerns. By acknowledging the historical roots of these practices, individuals can cultivate a deeper understanding of the principles guiding their pursuit of emotional wellness in today's society.

III. THE PSYCHOLOGY OF EMOTIONS

The psychology of emotions plays a crucial role in our overall mental health and well-being. Emotions are complex states of feeling that can significantly impact our thoughts, behaviors, and relationships. Understanding the underlying psychological mechanisms behind emotions is essential for effectively managing them and maintaining emotional wellness. Research in psychology has shown that emotions are influenced by a variety of factors, including biological, environmental, and cognitive components. By exploring the ways in which emotions are processed and regulated in the brain, individuals can gain insight into their emotional experiences and develop strategies for coping with challenging emotions. Additionally, cultivating emotional intelligence through self-awareness and empathy can lead to improved emotional regulation and healthier relationships. In conclusion, a comprehensive understanding of the psychology of emotions is vital for promoting mental health and emotional well-being.

BASIC EMOTIONS AND THEIR PSYCHOLOGICAL FUNCTIONS

Basic emotions play a pivotal role in shaping human behavior and cognitive processes. Emotions such as fear, anger, happiness, and sadness serve as fundamental mechanisms for survival and social interaction. Fear, for instance, helps individuals detect and respond to potential threats, thereby ensuring their safety and well-being. Anger, on the other hand, can motivate individuals to assert themselves and protect their boundaries. Happiness and sadness are essential for maintaining social bonds and processing complex emotional experiences. These basic emotions not only guide our actions but also influence our thought patterns and decision-making processes. By understanding the psychological functions of these emotions, individuals can learn to regulate and channel their emotional responses in a healthy and adaptive manner, ultimately leading to improved emotional well-being and mental health. In essence, basic emotions serve as a foundation for navigating the complexities of human experience and relationships.

THEORIES OF EMOTIONAL DEVELOPMENT

Theoretical perspectives on emotional development provide valuable insights into the complex processes involved in the shaping of emotions throughout the lifespan. From psychoanalytic theories emphasizing the role of early experiences and unconscious conflicts in emotional development to cognitive theories highlighting the role of cognition and social learning in shaping emotional responses, a range of perspectives offer diverse explanations. Developmental theories, such as attachment theory, suggest that early relationships and experiences play a crucial role in shaping emotional regulation and expression. In contrast, socioemotional selectivity theory posits that emotional goals and priorities shift across the lifespan in response to changing time horizons. By exploring these theories of emotional development, we can better understand the intricate interplay between individual differences, environmental factors, and social influences in shaping emotional well-being over time.

EMOTIONAL INTELLIGENCE AND ITS SIGNIFICANCE

Emotional intelligence plays a crucial role in promoting mental well-being and overall quality of life. Individuals with high emotional intelligence are better able to navigate through the complexities of interpersonal relationships, manage stress effectively, and make sound decisions based on empathy and self-awareness. By understanding and regulating their emotions, individuals can build resilience and cope with the challenges that life presents. Research has shown that emotional intelligence is linked to better mental health outcomes, such as reduced levels of anxiety and depression, higher levels of life satisfaction, and improved overall psychological functioning. Cultivating emotional intelligence through practices like mindfulness, self-reflection, and empathy training can enhance emotional regulation skills and improve interpersonal communication. Therefore, prioritizing the development of emotional intelligence is essential for maintaining a healthy mind and promoting emotional wellness in both personal and professional settings.

IV. BIOLOGICAL UNDERPINNINGS OF EMOTIONS

The biological underpinnings of emotions play a crucial role in understanding emotional wellness. Research has shown that various brain regions, such as the amygdala and prefrontal cortex, are involved in the processing and regulation of emotions. The amygdala, known as the brain's emotional center, is responsible for detecting potential threats and triggering the body's fight-or-flight response. On the other hand, the prefrontal cortex plays a key role in regulating emotions, decision-making, and social behavior. Dysfunction in these brain areas can lead to emotional disorders such as depression and anxiety. Additionally, neurotransmitters like serotonin and dopamine also play a significant role in regulating mood and emotions. Understanding the biological basis of emotions can lead to more effective interventions and treatments for individuals struggling with emotional dysregulation, ultimately improving their overall emotional well-being.

NEUROLOGICAL ASPECTS OF EMOTIONAL PROCESSING

The neural mechanisms involved in emotional processing play a crucial role in shaping human behavior and well-being. The amygdala, a key structure in the brain responsible for processing emotions, coordinates with other regions such as the prefrontal cortex to regulate emotional responses and decision-making. Studies have shown that individuals with damage to the amygdala exhibit deficits in recognizing emotions in others and struggle to appropriately respond to emotional cues. Furthermore, neuroimaging studies have revealed that individuals who practice mindfulness techniques show increased activity in regions related to emotional regulation, suggesting that mindfulness can enhance emotional processing and promote mental health. Understanding the neurological aspects of emotional processing is essential in developing interventions and therapies that target these brain regions to improve emotional well-being and overall psychological health.

HORMONAL INFLUENCES ON MOOD AND FEELINGS

Hormonal influences on mood and feelings play a crucial role in maintaining emotional wellness. The endocrine system regulates the release of hormones such as cortisol, adrenaline, and serotonin, which directly impact our mood and emotional state. For instance, cortisol, often referred to as the stress hormone, is released in response to perceived threats and can lead to feelings of anxiety and irritability if produced in excess. On the other hand, serotonin, known as the "feel-good" hormone, is responsible for feelings of happiness and well-being. Understanding how these hormones interact and fluctuate can help individuals better manage their emotional health. By adopting strategies such as stress management techniques, regular exercise, and a balanced diet, individuals can support hormonal balance and promote emotional stability. Ultimately, being aware of the hormonal influences on mood and feelings can empower individuals to take proactive steps towards enhancing their emotional well-being.

THE GUT-BRAIN AXIS AND EMOTIONAL HEALTH

The gut-brain axis plays a vital role in maintaining emotional health. Research has shown that the communication between the gut and the brain is bidirectional, with the gut influencing emotions and vice versa. The gut is home to a complex community of microorganisms known as the gut microbiota, which produce neurotransmitters that can affect mood and behavior. Furthermore, the gut microbiota also play a crucial role in regulating inflammation, which has been linked to various mental health disorders. Therapeutic strategies that target the gut-brain axis, such as probiotics and dietary interventions, have shown promise in improving emotional well-being. Understanding the intricate connection between the gut and the brain is essential for promoting emotional health and developing effective interventions for mental health disorders. By nurturing a healthy gut microbiome, individuals can potentially enhance their overall emotional wellness.

V. EMOTIONAL WELLNESS AND PHYSICAL HEALTH

The relationship between emotional wellness and physical health is a complex and multifaceted one that warrants careful examination. It is widely acknowledged that individuals who are emotionally well-adjusted tend to have better physical health outcomes. This correlation can be attributed to the bidirectional nature of the mind-body connection, where emotional states influence physical health and vice versa. Studies have shown that chronic stress, anxiety, and depression can have detrimental effects on the immune system, cardiovascular health, and overall well-being. On the other hand, individuals who cultivate emotional resilience, positive coping strategies, and a sense of well-being are more likely to experience better physical health outcomes. Therefore, it is imperative to address emotional wellness as an integral component of overall health and well-being, emphasizing the importance of holistic approaches to healthcare that consider the interconnectedness of mind and body.

THE CONNECTION BETWEEN EMOTIONAL AND PHYSICAL HEALTH

The connection between emotional and physical health is a topic that has gained significant attention in recent years. Research has shown that there is a strong link between the two, with emotional well-being playing a crucial role in overall physical health. When individuals experience chronic stress, anxiety, or depression, it can manifest in various physical symptoms such as headaches, digestive issues, and even cardiovascular problems. Additionally, negative emotions can weaken the immune system, making individuals more susceptible to illness. On the other hand, positive emotions like happiness and contentment can have a protective effect on the body, reducing inflammation and enhancing overall well-being. By addressing and managing emotions effectively, individuals can improve their physical health outcomes and overall quality of life. It is essential for healthcare providers to consider the emotional well-being of their patients as an integral part of holistic healthcare practices.

PSYCHOSOMATIC DISORDERS AND THEIR IMPLICATIONS

Psychosomatic disorders, often misunderstood and stigmatized, have profound implications for individuals' overall well-being. These conditions, where physical symptoms are caused or exacerbated by psychological factors, highlight the intricate connection between the mind and body. Understanding and addressing psychosomatic disorders is crucial in promoting emotional wellness as they can have a significant impact on one's quality of life. By recognizing the role of stress, trauma, and other psychological factors in the development of these disorders, healthcare professionals can tailor interventions that address both the physical and emotional aspects of the condition. Effective management of psychosomatic disorders involves a holistic approach that integrates psychological therapies, stress management techniques, and lifestyle modifications. By acknowledging the mind-body connection and providing comprehensive care, individuals with psychosomatic disorders can experience improved emotional well-being and overall health.

BENEFITS OF EMOTIONAL WELLNESS ON PHYSICAL WELL-BEING

Emotional wellness has been shown to have a profound impact on physical well-being, with numerous benefits that extend beyond simply improving mood and reducing stress. Research indicates that individuals with high levels of emotional wellness tend to have lower rates of chronic illnesses such as heart disease, diabetes, and autoimmune disorders. This connection can be attributed to the fact that emotional well-being is linked to healthier lifestyle choices, such as regular exercise, balanced nutrition, and adequate sleep. Furthermore, individuals with strong emotional wellness are better equipped to cope with stressors and adversity, thereby reducing the negative impact of chronic stress on the body. In essence, nurturing emotional wellness not only enhances mental health but also serves as a protective factor against physical ailments, providing a holistic approach to overall well-being. As such, prioritizing emotional wellness is essential for achieving optimal health outcomes.

VI. ASSESSING EMOTIONAL HEALTH

Assessing emotional health is a crucial aspect of overall well-being, as it directly impacts an individual's quality of life and ability to function effectively in daily activities. Various factors contribute to emotional health, including stress management, coping mechanisms, and interpersonal relationships. Evaluating emotional health involves assessing one's ability to regulate emotions, cope with stressors, and maintain positive relationships with others. This process often involves self-reflection, seeking feedback from trusted individuals, and engaging in therapeutic interventions if necessary. By actively assessing emotional health, individuals can identify areas of improvement and work towards enhancing their emotional well-being. This proactive approach can lead to greater resilience, improved self-esteem, and a more balanced overall mental state. Ultimately, by prioritizing the assessment of emotional health, individuals can cultivate a healthier mindset and lay the foundation for a more fulfilling and satisfying life.

TOOLS AND METHODS FOR EVALUATING EMOTIONAL WELLNESS

Tools and methods for evaluating emotional wellness play a crucial role in assessing an individual's overall mental health. Beginning with self-report measures such as questionnaires and surveys, these tools provide a glimpse into an individual's subjective experience of emotions. However, relying solely on self-report data has limitations, as it may be influenced by bias or misinterpretation. Moving to more objective measures, methods like psychophysiological assessments, such as heart rate variability and electrodermal activity, offer a more quantifiable way to gauge emotional states. Additionally, neuroimaging techniques like fMRI can provide valuable insights into the neural correlates of emotional experiences. By integrating both subjective and objective measures, a comprehensive evaluation of emotional wellness can be achieved, leading to more precise interventions and tailored treatments for those struggling with emotional well-being.

SELF-ASSESSMENT TECHNIQUES

Self-assessment techniques are crucial tools for fostering emotional wellness. These methods allow individuals to introspect and evaluate their thoughts, feelings, and behaviors, thereby gaining a deeper understanding of themselves. By engaging in self-reflection, individuals can identify areas for growth and pinpoint triggers for negative emotions, enabling them to develop coping strategies and implement positive changes. Self-assessment techniques also promote self-awareness and self-acceptance, leading to improved self-esteem and a greater sense of inner peace. Moreover, by regularly assessing one's emotional state, individuals can track their progress towards emotional well-being and adjust their strategies as needed. Overall, self-assessment techniques serve as invaluable resources for enhancing emotional intelligence and overall mental health, making them essential components of a holistic approach to wellness.

PROFESSIONAL ASSESSMENT AND DIAGNOSIS

Professional assessment and diagnosis play a crucial role in ensuring individuals receive the appropriate treatment and support for their mental health concerns. It is essential for healthcare professionals to conduct a thorough evaluation of a patient's symptoms, history, and current challenges to make an accurate diagnosis. This process involves utilizing standardized assessment tools, conducting interviews, and collaborating with other healthcare providers to gather comprehensive information. In addition to identifying the specific mental health condition, a professional diagnosis can guide the development of a personalized treatment plan tailored to the individual's needs. Furthermore, an accurate diagnosis helps to reduce the risk of misdiagnosis and ensures that patients receive the most effective interventions. Overall, professional assessment and diagnosis are indispensable components of mental health care that enable individuals to access the appropriate support and resources for their emotional well-being.

VII. COMMON EMOTIONAL DISORDERS

Common emotional disorders such as anxiety, depression, and PTSD are prevalent in today's society, affecting individuals of all ages and backgrounds. These disorders can significantly impair one's quality of life and functioning, leading to negative consequences in various areas such as work, relationships, and overall well-being. Anxiety disorders, characterized by excessive worrying and fear, can be debilitating and interfere with daily activities. Depression, marked by persistent sadness and loss of interest, can make even simple tasks seem overwhelming. Post-Traumatic Stress Disorder (PTSD) can result from exposure to a traumatic event, causing intrusive memories, avoidance behaviors, and heightened arousal. Recognizing the symptoms and seeking appropriate treatment is crucial in managing these emotional disorders effectively. Through therapy, medication, and lifestyle changes, individuals can learn to cope with and overcome these challenges, ultimately promoting emotional wellness and a healthy mind.

OVERVIEW OF ANXIETY DISORDERS

Anxiety disorders encompass a range of conditions characterized by overwhelming feelings of fear, worry, and apprehension that can interfere with daily functioning. These disorders include generalized anxiety disorder, panic disorder, social anxiety disorder, and specific phobias, among others. Individuals with anxiety disorders may experience symptoms such as rapid heart rate, sweating, trembling, and a sense of impending doom. These conditions can be debilitating, affecting one's personal relationships, work performance, and overall quality of life. While some level of anxiety is a normal human experience, excessive and persistent anxiety can be detrimental to one's well-being. Understanding the underlying causes and triggers of anxiety disorders is crucial for effective treatment and management. Employing a combination of therapy, medication, and lifestyle changes can help individuals with anxiety disorders lead more fulfilling and balanced lives.

DEPRESSIVE DISORDERS AND THEIR IMPACT

Depressive disorders, such as major depressive disorder and persistent depressive disorder, have a significant impact on individuals' emotional well-being and overall quality of life. These disorders are characterized by persistent feelings of sadness, hopelessness, and worthlessness that can interfere with daily functioning and relationships. Research suggests that depressive disorders are associated with an increased risk of developing other mental health conditions, such as anxiety disorders and substance abuse. Additionally, individuals with depressive disorders may experience physical symptoms like fatigue, changes in appetite, and sleep disturbances. The impact of these disorders extends beyond the individual, affecting family members, friends, and colleagues. Therefore, it is crucial for healthcare providers to accurately diagnose and effectively treat depressive disorders to improve outcomes and prevent long-term consequences on individuals' mental health and well-being.

OTHER PREVALENT EMOTIONAL HEALTH ISSUES

Other prevalent emotional health issues that can significantly impact an individual's overall well-being include anxiety disorders, eating disorders, and substance abuse. Anxiety disorders, such as generalized anxiety disorder and panic disorder, can lead to chronic worry and fear, affecting daily functioning. Similarly, eating disorders like anorexia nervosa and bulimia nervosa can result in severe physical and emotional consequences, including malnutrition and low self-esteem. Substance abuse, including alcohol and drug addiction, can also have profound effects on mental health, leading to mood disorders and impaired cognitive function. Addressing these emotional health issues requires a comprehensive approach that includes therapy, medication, and lifestyle modifications. By recognizing and addressing these prevalent emotional health issues, individuals can take steps towards achieving emotional wellness and improving their overall quality of life.

VIII. THE ROLE OF STRESS IN EMOTIONAL WELLNESS

In exploring the relationship between stress and emotional wellness, it is crucial to consider the impact of chronic stress on mental health. Research has shown that prolonged exposure to stress can lead to the development of anxiety, depression, and other mood disorders. Individuals experiencing high levels of stress may struggle to regulate their emotions effectively, leading to heightened reactivity and difficulty in managing daily stressors. However, it is important to recognize that not all stress is detrimental to emotional wellness. Acute stress, when managed effectively, can actually enhance resilience and improve coping mechanisms. Therefore, it is essential to distinguish between healthy and unhealthy forms of stress, and develop strategies to mitigate the negative effects of chronic stress on emotional well-being. By promoting stress management techniques, individuals can cultivate a more balanced and resilient emotional state, ultimately promoting overall wellness.

UNDERSTANDING STRESS AND ITS EFFECTS

Understanding stress and its effects is crucial in maintaining emotional wellness. Stress can manifest physically, emotionally, and behaviorally, impacting overall well-being. Physiologically, stress triggers the release of cortisol, the body's primary stress hormone, which can lead to various health issues such as high blood pressure and weakened immune function. Emotionally, stress can cause feelings of anxiety, depression, and irritability, affecting one's mental health. Behaviorally, stress can result in changes in eating habits, sleep patterns, and social interactions. Recognizing the signs of stress and its effects is the first step in managing and mitigating its impact. By developing coping strategies, such as practicing mindfulness, engaging in physical activity, and seeking social support, individuals can build resilience and enhance their emotional well-being. Overall, a deep understanding of stress and its effects is essential for promoting emotional wellness and maintaining a healthy mind.

STRESS MANAGEMENT TECHNIQUES

One crucial aspect of maintaining emotional wellness is the implementation of effective stress management techniques. Individuals can employ various strategies to cope with stress and prevent its negative effects on mental health. These techniques may include mindfulness practices, relaxation exercises, physical activity, and seeking social support. Mindfulness, such as meditation and deep breathing exercises, can help individuals stay present and reduce anxiety. Engaging in regular physical activity is also essential, as it can release endorphins and improve mood. Additionally, cultivating strong social connections and seeking support from friends, family, or professionals can provide a sense of belonging and comfort during times of stress. By incorporating a combination of these stress management techniques into daily routines, individuals can better manage their stress levels and promote emotional well-being.

LONG-TERM CONSEQUENCES OF UNMANAGED STRESS

The long-term consequences of unmanaged stress can have significant negative effects on both physical and mental health. Research has shown that chronic stress can lead to a myriad of health issues, including increased risk of heart disease, obesity, and diabetes. Furthermore, prolonged exposure to stress hormones such as cortisol can impair cognitive function and memory, impacting one's ability to focus and make rational decisions. Over time, this can also contribute to the development of mental health disorders such as anxiety and depression. It is crucial for individuals to recognize the importance of managing stress through various techniques such as mindfulness, exercise, and therapy to prevent these detrimental long-term consequences. By prioritizing emotional wellness and implementing healthy coping mechanisms, individuals can mitigate the damaging effects of stress and maintain a balanced and healthy mind.

IX. COPING MECHANISMS AND STRATEGIES

In discussing coping mechanisms and strategies for emotional well-being, it is crucial to explore a range of healthy practices that individuals can utilize in times of stress or adversity. One effective coping mechanism is mindfulness meditation, which involves focusing on the present moment in a non-judgmental way. This practice can help individuals cultivate self-awareness and reduce feelings of anxiety or depression. Additionally, engaging in regular physical exercise can have a significant impact on mental health by releasing endorphins and promoting overall well-being. Seeking support from friends, family members, or mental health professionals is another valuable coping strategy that can provide individuals with the encouragement and guidance needed to navigate challenging emotions. By incorporating a variety of coping mechanisms into their daily routines, individuals can build resilience and foster a healthy mindset for long-term emotional wellness.

ADAPTIVE VS. MALADAPTIVE COPING

Adaptive coping mechanisms are essential for promoting emotional wellness, as they are functional strategies individuals utilize to manage stressors effectively and maintain psychological well-being. These include problem-solving, seeking social support, and engaging in activities that promote relaxation and self-care. On the other hand, maladaptive coping strategies can be detrimental to mental health when they involve avoidance, substance abuse, or engaging in self-destructive behavior. It is crucial for individuals to recognize the difference between adaptive and maladaptive coping mechanisms and actively work towards cultivating healthier ways of managing stressors. By developing adaptive coping skills, individuals can build resilience, enhance emotional regulation, and improve overall psychological functioning. Ultimately, choosing adaptive coping strategies over maladaptive ones can lead to a healthier and more balanced emotional state, contributing to long-term emotional wellness.

BUILDING RESILIENCE

Building resilience is a critical component of achieving emotional wellness. It involves developing the capacity to adapt to challenges, bounce back from adversity, and thrive in the face of difficult circumstances. One key aspect of building resilience is through fostering a growth mindset, which allows individuals to view setbacks as opportunities for growth rather than insurmountable obstacles. Additionally, practicing self-care and prioritizing mental health can help build resilience by ensuring individuals have the resources and support they need to navigate tough times. Moreover, building strong social connections and a support network can provide a sense of belonging and stability, boosting resilience in times of need. Ultimately, building resilience is a multifaceted process that requires intentional effort and self-awareness, but the rewards of increased emotional strength and well-being are invaluable.

COPING WITH LOSS AND GRIEF

When individuals experience loss and grief, it is essential to have effective coping mechanisms in place to navigate the challenging emotions that come with such experiences. One approach to coping is through the practice of mindfulness and self-reflection. By allowing oneself to acknowledge and sit with the feelings of loss without judgment, individuals can begin to process and eventually heal from their grief. Seeking support from friends, family, or a mental health professional can also be beneficial in providing a safe space to express emotions and receive guidance. Additionally, engaging in self-care activities such as exercise, journaling, or engaging in hobbies can help to channel energy positively and promote emotional well-being. Overall, developing a toolbox of coping strategies tailored to one's needs can facilitate the healing process and promote emotional wellness in the face of loss and grief.

X. MINDFULNESS AND EMOTIONAL HEALTH

Mindfulness has shown promise in enhancing emotional health by cultivating awareness of one's thoughts, feelings, and sensations without judgment. This practice allows individuals to develop greater emotional intelligence, which can lead to improved self-regulation and the ability to navigate challenging situations with resilience. By honing their mindfulness skills, individuals can enhance their capacity to manage stress, anxiety, and depression, and cultivate a more positive outlook on life. Research indicates that mindfulness-based interventions can reduce symptoms of emotional distress and promote overall well-being. Incorporating mindfulness into daily routines can foster emotional balance, increased self-awareness, and a deeper connection to one's inner experiences. By integrating mindfulness practices into our lives, we can enhance our emotional health and build a solid foundation for overall wellness.

PRINCIPLES OF MINDFULNESS

Mindfulness is a foundational principle that underpins emotional wellness, as it involves being fully present and engaged in the present moment without judgment. This practice encourages individuals to cultivate awareness of their thoughts, emotions, and sensations, allowing them to respond to situations with clarity and compassion. By developing mindfulness, individuals can better manage stress, reduce anxiety, and enhance overall well-being. Research suggests that mindfulness can positively impact brain function, improve emotional regulation, and promote resilience in the face of challenges. Through mindful practices such as meditation, deep breathing, and body scans, individuals can train their minds to focus on the present moment and let go of distractions. Incorporating mindfulness into daily life can lead to increased self-awareness, emotional intelligence, and a greater sense of inner peace. By embracing the principles of mindfulness, individuals can cultivate a healthy mind and navigate life's ups and downs with grace and resilience.

MINDFULNESS PRACTICES FOR EMOTIONAL REGULATION

Mindfulness practices offer a promising approach for enhancing emotional regulation. By cultivating a non-judgmental and present-focused awareness, individuals can develop the capacity to observe and acknowledge their emotions without becoming overwhelmed by them. This ability to step back and observe one's emotional responses can lead to greater self-control and a more adaptive regulation of emotions. Research supports the efficacy of mindfulness techniques in reducing emotional reactivity and promoting emotional well-being. Studies have shown that regular practice of mindfulness can lead to changes in brain regions associated with emotion regulation, such as the amygdala and prefrontal cortex. Additionally, mindfulness interventions have been shown to be effective in reducing symptoms of anxiety, depression, and other mood disorders. Incorporating mindfulness practices into daily routines can help individuals develop a healthier relationship with their emotions, leading to improved overall emotional wellness.

RESEARCH ON MINDFULNESS AND MENTAL HEALTH OUTCOMES

Research on mindfulness and mental health outcomes has gained significant attention in recent years. Studies have shown that practicing mindfulness can lead to reduced symptoms of anxiety, depression, and stress. By cultivating present-moment awareness and nonjudgmental acceptance, individuals can improve their emotional well-being and cognitive functioning. Mindfulness-based interventions have been found to be effective in treating a variety of mental health conditions, such as post-traumatic stress disorder and substance abuse. Additionally, mindfulness practices have been linked to enhanced self-regulation skills and overall psychological resilience. The integration of mindfulness techniques into therapy and self-care routines can provide individuals with valuable tools for addressing emotional challenges and promoting long-term mental health. As the body of research continues to grow, it is clear that mindfulness holds great promise for improving mental health outcomes and enhancing overall well-being.

XI. COGNITIVE BEHAVIORAL APPROACHES

Cognitive behavioral approaches have gained significant popularity in the field of psychology due to their effectiveness in treating a wide range of mental health issues. This therapeutic technique focuses on identifying and changing negative thought patterns and behaviors that contribute to emotional distress. By helping individuals recognize and challenge their irrational beliefs, cognitive behavioral therapy (CBT) empowers them to develop healthier coping strategies and achieve lasting improvements in their mental well-being. Research has shown that CBT is particularly effective in managing conditions such as anxiety disorders, depression, and PTSD. The structured nature of CBT makes it suitable for individuals seeking a practical and goal-oriented approach to therapy. With its emphasis on collaboration between therapist and client, cognitive behavioral approaches provide a valuable framework for promoting emotional wellness and resilience in individuals seeking to enhance their mental health.

FUNDAMENTALS OF COGNITIVE-BEHAVIORAL THERAPY

The fundamentals of CBT serve as a cornerstone in promoting emotional wellness and mental health. CBT operates on the premise that thoughts, feelings, and behaviors are interconnected, and that positive changes in one area can lead to improvements in the others. By identifying and challenging negative thought patterns, individuals can learn to reframe their beliefs and adopt healthier coping mechanisms. This proactive approach empowers individuals to take control of their mental health and develop practical skills to manage stress, anxiety, and other emotional challenges. Through the use of evidence-based techniques such as cognitive restructuring and behavioral experiments, CBT equips individuals with the tools needed to navigate through life's difficulties with resilience and adaptability. In essence, the principles of CBT underscore the importance of self-awareness, critical thinking, and personal agency in fostering a healthy mind and emotional well-being.

CBT TECHNIQUES FOR EMOTIONAL WELLNESS

CBT techniques have shown significant efficacy in promoting emotional wellness. By focusing on identifying and challenging negative thought patterns, CBT empowers individuals to reframe their thinking, leading to improved mood and emotional regulation. Through techniques such as cognitive restructuring, individuals can learn to replace irrational beliefs with more rational and constructive ones, ultimately fostering a more positive outlook on life. Additionally, behavioral activation techniques encourage individuals to engage in rewarding activities that bring them joy and satisfaction, helping to combat feelings of depression and anxiety. CBT also equips individuals with coping skills and stress management strategies, enabling them to navigate challenging situations with resilience and adaptability. Overall, the integration of CBT techniques into mental health treatment plans can lead to lasting emotional well-being and improved overall quality of life.

EFFECTIVENESS OF CBT FOR VARIOUS EMOTIONAL DISORDERS

Numerous studies have shown the effectiveness of CBT in treating various emotional disorders like anxiety, depression, and post-traumatic stress disorder. CBT is based on the principle that our thoughts, feelings, and behaviors are interconnected, and by changing our thought patterns, we can effectively change our emotional responses. Research has demonstrated that CBT can help individuals develop coping strategies, reframe negative thought patterns, and challenge maladaptive beliefs. Additionally, CBT has been found to be as effective as medication in treating certain emotional disorders, with the added benefit of equipping individuals with long-lasting skills to manage their symptoms independently. Overall, the evidence supports the use of CBT as a valuable therapeutic approach for addressing a wide range of emotional disorders, promoting positive outcomes and enhancing emotional wellness in individuals seeking treatment.

XII. THE IMPACT OF LIFESTYLE ON EMOTIONAL WELLNESS

The impact of lifestyle on emotional wellness is a crucial aspect to consider in maintaining overall mental health. Lifestyle choices such as diet, exercise, sleep patterns, and stress management can all significantly influence an individual's emotional well-being. Engaging in regular physical activity has been shown to boost mood, reduce anxiety, and alleviate symptoms of depression. Additionally, a balanced diet rich in nutrients can support brain health and contribute to a more stable emotional state. Adequate sleep is essential for emotional regulation and cognitive function, while effective stress management techniques such as mindfulness practices or therapy can help individuals cope with life's challenges. By making conscious and intentional lifestyle choices, individuals can enhance their emotional wellness and improve their overall quality of life. It is important to recognize the interconnectedness of lifestyle factors and emotional well-being in order to cultivate a healthy mind.

DIET AND NUTRITION

Diet and nutrition play a fundamental role in promoting emotional wellness. Research shows that maintaining a balanced and nutrient-rich diet can positively impact mood and mental health. For example, consuming foods rich in omega-3 fatty acids, such as salmon or chia seeds, has been linked to decreased symptoms of depression and anxiety. Additionally, foods high in antioxidants, like berries and leafy greens, can help reduce oxidative stress and inflammation in the brain, which are often associated with mood disorders. On the other hand, diets high in processed foods, sugar, and saturated fats have been shown to increase the risk of developing mental health issues. Therefore, individuals should prioritize whole, fresh foods in their diet to support their emotional well-being. By making conscious choices about what they eat, individuals can nourish both their bodies and minds for optimal health and happiness.

EXERCISE AND PHYSICAL ACTIVITY

Exercise and physical activity play a crucial role in promoting emotional wellness. Engaging in regular physical activity has been linked to improved mood, reduced stress and anxiety levels, and better overall mental health. Exercise helps release endorphins, often referred to as "feel-good" hormones, which can elevate mood and reduce feelings of depression. Furthermore, physical activity can serve as a healthy coping mechanism for managing stress and negative emotions. Incorporating exercise into one's daily routine can lead to increased self-esteem, improved cognitive function, and a heightened sense of well-being. Research has shown that individuals who prioritize physical activity as part of their lifestyle experience better emotional resilience and are better equipped to handle life's challenges. Overall, exercise and physical activity are integral components of maintaining a healthy mind and emotional well-being.

SLEEP PATTERNS AND EMOTIONAL HEALTH

Sleep patterns play a crucial role in emotional health as they affect mood regulation and cognitive functioning. Adequate sleep allows for the consolidation of memories and the processing of emotions, leading to improved mood stability and stress management. Disruptions in sleep patterns, such as insomnia or sleep apnea, have been linked to increased risk of developing mood disorders like anxiety and depression. Additionally, poor sleep quality can exacerbate emotional dysregulation and impair decision-making abilities. Therefore, it is essential to prioritize healthy sleep habits to support optimal emotional well-being. By maintaining a consistent sleep schedule, creating a restful sleep environment, and practicing relaxation techniques before bedtime, individuals can improve their emotional health and enhance their overall quality of life. Ultimately, the relationship between sleep patterns and emotional health underscores the importance of addressing sleep disturbances as part of a comprehensive approach to emotional wellness.

XIII. THE INFLUENCE OF SOCIAL RELATIONSHIPS

Social relationships play a crucial role in shaping our emotional wellness. The interactions we have with others can have a profound impact on our mental health, influencing our moods, self-esteem, and overall well-being. Positive relationships provide a sense of belonging and support, contributing to feelings of happiness and fulfillment. On the other hand, toxic relationships can lead to stress, anxiety, and even depression. It is important to cultivate healthy relationships and surround ourselves with people who uplift and encourage us. Building strong social connections can enhance resilience, decrease feelings of loneliness, and improve our overall mental health. By nurturing positive relationships and setting boundaries with negative influences, we can create a more supportive and emotionally fulfilling environment for ourselves. Ultimately, the quality of our social interactions greatly influences our emotional well-being and should be a priority in maintaining a healthy mind.

SOCIAL SUPPORT NETWORKS

Social support networks are essential for maintaining emotional wellness. These networks provide individuals with a sense of belonging, emotional validation, and practical assistance during times of need. Research has shown that individuals with strong social support systems are better equipped to cope with stress, anxiety, and depression. Family, friends, and community resources can offer different types of support, including emotional support, instrumental support, informational support, and appraisal support. By nurturing these relationships and cultivating a diverse network of support, individuals can build resilience and enhance their overall well-being. In times of crisis or emotional distress, having a strong support system can provide a buffer against negative outcomes and facilitate emotional recovery. Cultivating and maintaining social support networks should be a priority for individuals seeking to achieve and maintain emotional wellness.

THE ROLE OF INTIMACY AND EMOTIONAL CONNECTION

Intimacy and emotional connection play vital roles in promoting emotional wellness. At the core of healthy relationships, intimacy fosters a sense of closeness, trust, and vulnerability between individuals. This emotional bond can provide a source of support, validation, and empathy, leading to improved mental health outcomes. Research has shown that individuals who feel emotionally connected to others are more likely to experience lower levels of stress, anxiety, and depression. Moreover, intimate relationships have been linked to increased feelings of self-worth and life satisfaction. Cultivating emotional connections can also enhance communication skills, conflict resolution abilities, and overall resilience in the face of challenges. In sum, fostering intimacy and emotional connection is essential for promoting emotional well-being and building strong, fulfilling relationships.

NAVIGATING TOXIC RELATIONSHIPS

To effectively navigate toxic relationships, individuals must first recognize the signs of toxicity, whether it be manipulation, emotional abuse, or lack of boundaries. This awareness is crucial in establishing healthy boundaries and making informed decisions about the relationship's future. Once the toxic behavior is identified, it is essential to communicate openly and honestly with the other party, expressing concerns and setting clear expectations. However, if the relationship continues to be harmful despite efforts to address the issues, it may be necessary to consider ending the relationship for the sake of one's emotional well-being. Ultimately, prioritizing self-care and surrounding oneself with supportive and positive influences are key in fostering emotional wellness and breaking free from toxic dynamics. By taking proactive steps to address toxic relationships, individuals can pave the way for a healthier and more fulfilling life.

XIV. EMOTIONAL WELLNESS IN THE WORKPLACE

Emotional wellness in the workplace is a critical aspect of organizational health, as it can significantly impact employee productivity, job satisfaction, and overall success. Creating a supportive work environment that prioritizes emotional well-being can lead to reduced stress levels, improved communication among colleagues, and increased motivation to tackle challenges. Companies that invest in programs and initiatives aimed at enhancing emotional wellness often see higher levels of employee engagement and lower rates of absenteeism. Implementing strategies such as regular check-ins with employees, providing resources for mental health support, and promoting work-life balance can contribute to a positive and resilient workforce. By recognizing the importance of emotional wellness in the workplace, organizations can foster a more positive and productive work culture that benefits both employees and the overall bottom line.

WORK-LIFE BALANCE AND EMOTIONAL HEALTH

Work-life balance is crucial for maintaining emotional health, as constant work demands can lead to burnout and increased stress levels. Finding time to engage in activities that bring joy and relaxation outside of work can help individuals recharge and prevent emotional exhaustion. In today's fast-paced world, where technology blurs the boundaries between work and personal life, it is essential to set clear boundaries and prioritize self-care. Incorporating regular exercise, mindfulness practices, and social connections into one's routine can improve emotional well-being and overall satisfaction with life. By striving for a healthy work-life balance, individuals can better manage their emotions, reduce feelings of overwhelm, and cultivate a sense of fulfillment in both their professional and personal lives. Prioritizing emotional health through work-life balance is not only beneficial for individuals but also contributes to a more productive and harmonious society.

MANAGING WORKPLACE STRESS

Effective management of workplace stress is crucial for maintaining employee well-being and productivity. To tackle this issue, organizations should implement strategies that address the root causes of stress, such as excessive workload, lack of autonomy, and poor work-life balance. Providing employees with the necessary resources and support to handle stress is also essential. This can include training programs on stress management techniques, access to mental health resources, and fostering a culture that values work-life balance and encourages open communication. Additionally, creating a supportive work environment where employees feel empowered to speak up about their stressors without fear of judgment can help prevent stress from escalating. By prioritizing the mental health of employees and implementing proactive measures to manage workplace stress, organizations can create a healthier and more productive work environment.

PROMOTING EMOTIONAL WELLNESS IN ORGANIZATIONAL CULTURE

Promoting emotional wellness in organizational culture is essential for creating a positive work environment that fosters productivity and employee satisfaction. By implementing strategies such as regular check-ins with employees, offering mental health resources, and encouraging a work-life balance, organizations can prioritize the emotional well-being of their staff. When employees feel supported and valued, they are more likely to be engaged in their work and perform at a higher level. Additionally, promoting emotional wellness can lead to reduced absenteeism, lower turnover rates, and overall improved morale within the organization. Ultimately, investing in the emotional wellness of employees not only benefits individuals but also contributes to the overall success and sustainability of the organization as a whole. Therefore, creating a culture that prioritizes emotional wellness is a proactive and beneficial approach for organizations to take in promoting a healthy work environment.

XV. TECHNOLOGY AND EMOTIONAL WELLNESS

The intersection of technology and emotional wellness is a complex and evolving subject that requires careful consideration in today's digital age. While advancements in technology have provided numerous benefits for society, such as increased communication and access to information, there is a growing concern about the impact on individual emotional well-being. Excessive screen time, social media usage, and constant connectivity have been linked to higher levels of stress, anxiety, and depression. It is crucial for individuals to establish boundaries and prioritize self-care practices to maintain a healthy balance between technology use and emotional wellness. Incorporating mindfulness techniques, setting limits on screen time, and engaging in face-to-face interactions can help mitigate the negative effects of technology on mental health. By being mindful of our technology consumption and making intentional choices, we can cultivate a healthier relationship with technology and promote emotional well-being in the digital age.

DIGITAL CONNECTIVITY AND ITS EFFECTS ON EMOTIONS

Digital connectivity has undoubtedly revolutionized the way we communicate and interact with others, but its effects on emotions are complex and multifaceted. On one hand, the constant barrage of notifications and messages can lead to feelings of overwhelm and anxiety, as individuals struggle to keep up with the demands of their online lives. On the other hand, digital connectivity also provides opportunities for social support and connection, which can have a positive impact on emotional well-being. However, the relentless comparison and competition that often characterize social media platforms can also lead to feelings of inadequacy and low self-esteem. Therefore, it is crucial for individuals to cultivate mindfulness and self-awareness in their online interactions to mitigate the negative effects of digital connectivity on emotions and promote a healthy mind. By being intentional about their online presence and setting boundaries around their use of technology, individuals can harness the benefits of digital connectivity while safeguarding their emotional well-being.

THE USE OF TECHNOLOGY IN MENTAL HEALTH INTERVENTIONS

The use of technology in mental health interventions has shown great promise in providing accessible and effective support for individuals struggling with various mental health challenges. Advances in telehealth, mobile apps, virtual reality, and artificial intelligence have opened up new avenues for delivering therapeutic interventions and monitoring mental well-being. These technological tools can enhance the reach and impact of mental health services, particularly in reaching underserved populations or those facing barriers to traditional in-person therapy. By leveraging technology, mental health professionals can tailor interventions to meet individual needs, track progress in real-time, and provide ongoing support beyond traditional therapy sessions. However, it is essential to carefully consider ethical concerns, privacy issues, and the potential limitations of technology in delivering mental health care. As technology continues to evolve, integrating evidence-based practices with innovative technological solutions can revolutionize the field of mental health and improve outcomes for individuals seeking support.

THE RISKS OF TECHNOLOGY ADDICTION

The risks of technology addiction are becoming increasingly evident in today's society. The allure of constant connectivity and instant gratification offered by smartphones, social media, and other digital platforms can lead to detrimental effects on one's mental health. Excessive use of technology can result in feelings of anxiety, loneliness, and depression as individuals become overly reliant on virtual interactions while neglecting real-life relationships and experiences. Moreover, the cycle of dopamine hits from notifications and likes can create a dangerous dependence, akin to that of substance abuse. As a result, it is crucial to recognize the signs of technology addiction and take proactive steps to set boundaries, prioritize real-world connections, and cultivate mindfulness in order to safeguard our emotional well-being in the digital age. By acknowledging and addressing the risks of technology addiction, individuals can work towards achieving a healthier balance in their relationship with technology.

XVI. CULTURAL CONSIDERATIONS IN EMOTIONAL WELLNESS

Cultural Considerations in Emotional Wellness play a crucial role in shaping individuals' mental health and overall well-being. Understanding how cultural background, beliefs, traditions, and societal norms influence one's emotional experiences is paramount in providing effective support and intervention. By acknowledging and respecting diverse cultural perspectives, mental health professionals can tailor their interventions to be more culturally sensitive and relevant. It is essential to recognize that emotional wellness is not a one-size-fits-all concept and that different cultures may perceive and express emotions in unique ways. By incorporating cultural considerations into therapeutic practices and mental health policies, we can promote a more inclusive and comprehensive approach to emotional well-being. Ultimately, embracing diversity in emotional wellness allows for more effective support and treatment for individuals from various cultural backgrounds, leading to better outcomes in mental health care.

CULTURAL DEFINITIONS AND EXPRESSIONS OF EMOTIONS

Cultural definitions and expressions of emotions play a crucial role in shaping individual and societal understanding of mental wellness. Cultures vary in their norms, values, and beliefs about emotions, influencing how individuals perceive, label, and regulate their emotional experiences. For instance, some cultures may prioritize the expression of positive emotions while suppressing negative ones, leading to emotional suppression and potential psychological issues. In contrast, other cultures may value the open expression of a wide range of emotions, promoting emotional authenticity and psychological well-being. Understanding these cultural influences is essential in promoting emotional wellness on a global scale. By recognizing and respecting diverse cultural definitions and expressions of emotions, mental health professionals can provide more culturally sensitive and effective interventions to support individuals' emotional well-being across different cultural backgrounds.

CROSS-CULTURAL APPROACHES TO EMOTIONAL HEALTH

Cross-cultural approaches to emotional health are essential in understanding how cultural differences impact individual well-being. By recognizing that emotional health is not solely determined by biological factors but also influenced by sociocultural contexts, we can develop more effective interventions and support systems. Cultures vary in their norms, values, and expressions of emotions, leading to diverse perspectives on what constitutes emotional well-being. Therefore, a one-size-fits-all approach to mental health may not effectively address the needs of individuals from different cultural backgrounds. Cross-cultural approaches allow for a more nuanced understanding of emotional health, taking into account the unique cultural factors that shape individuals' experiences. By integrating cultural sensitivity and awareness into mental health practices, we can promote emotional well-being in a more holistic and inclusive manner. A comprehensive understanding of cross-cultural approaches to emotional health is crucial for addressing the diverse needs of individuals in today's multicultural societies.

ADAPTING WELLNESS PRACTICES TO DIVERSE POPULATIONS

Adapting wellness practices to diverse populations is a critical aspect of promoting emotional well-being across different communities. Recognizing the unique backgrounds, beliefs, and needs of various groups is essential in tailoring effective wellness interventions. Culturally sensitive approaches that consider the values and traditions of diverse populations can enhance engagement and improve outcomes. By acknowledging and respecting cultural differences, healthcare providers can build trust and rapport with individuals seeking support for their mental health. Moreover, adapting wellness practices to diverse populations can help address disparities in access to care and outcomes within marginalized communities. It is imperative to collaborate with community leaders and organizations to ensure that wellness programs are inclusive and culturally competent. Ultimately, by embracing diversity and inclusivity in wellness initiatives, we can work towards fostering a more equitable and thriving society.

XVII. GENDER AND EMOTIONAL WELLNESS

Gender plays a significant role in shaping emotional wellness, with societal expectations and norms often influencing how individuals express and regulate their emotions. Men and women may experience different pressures and constraints when it comes to emotional expression, leading to disparities in mental health outcomes. Research suggests that men may be socialized to suppress their emotions, leading to higher rates of depression and suicide. On the other hand, women may face stigma for being too emotional or sensitive, impacting their self-esteem and well-being. It is crucial to recognize these gendered patterns and work towards creating a more inclusive and supportive environment for individuals of all gender identities to express their emotions authentically. By challenging traditional gender norms and promoting emotional intelligence in both men and women, we can foster a society that prioritizes mental health and emotional well-being for all.

GENDER DIFFERENCES IN EMOTIONAL EXPRESSION AND PROCESSING

Gender differences in emotional expression and processing have long been a subject of interest in psychology and sociology. Studies have shown that men and women tend to exhibit different patterns of emotional behavior, with women being more likely to express their emotions openly and seek social support, while men may be more inclined to suppress their feelings. These differences are often attributed to socialization processes, with cultural norms dictating acceptable modes of emotional expression for each gender. Additionally, research has suggested that biological factors, such as hormonal influences, may also play a role in shaping these gender differences. Understanding these differences is crucial for promoting emotional wellness, as it can help individuals recognize and navigate their own emotional experiences more effectively. By acknowledging and embracing these differences, we can create a more inclusive and understanding environment for all individuals to thrive emotionally.

SOCIETAL EXPECTATIONS AND THEIR IMPACT ON EMOTIONAL HEALTH

Societal expectations play a significant role in shaping individuals' emotional health. From a young age, people are bombarded with messages about how they should look, act, and feel. These expectations can create pressure to conform to certain standards, leading to feelings of inadequacy, anxiety, and depression. In a society that values productivity and success, individuals may experience heightened stress levels as they strive to meet these expectations. Moreover, the fear of judgment or rejection for not meeting societal norms can further contribute to emotional distress. To promote emotional wellness, it is crucial to challenge and redefine these expectations, focusing instead on self-acceptance, self-care, and authenticity. By fostering a culture that embraces diversity and individuality, we can create a more inclusive and supportive environment that prioritizes mental well-being over societal standards.

ADDRESSING GENDER-SPECIFIC EMOTIONAL HEALTH NEEDS

Addressing gender-specific emotional health needs is crucial in promoting overall emotional wellness. Research has shown that men and women may experience and express emotions differently, leading to unique mental health concerns. For instance, men are less likely to seek help for emotional issues due to societal expectations that dictate they should be tough and stoic. As a result, interventions tailored to men's needs, such as promoting emotional expression and seeking support, are essential. On the other hand, women may face challenges related to societal pressures, body image issues, and gender-based violence, which require specialized approaches. By recognizing and addressing these gender-specific emotional health needs, mental health professionals can provide more effective and targeted support to individuals. Ultimately, creating inclusive and comprehensive mental health services that consider gender differences can lead to better outcomes and improved emotional well-being for all.

XVIII. THE ROLE OF EDUCATION IN EMOTIONAL WELLNESS

The role of education in emotional wellness in the XVIII century was pivotal in shaping individuals' mental health. During this era, the Enlightenment period brought a renewed focus on education as a means to cultivate emotional intelligence and well-being. Educational institutions emphasized not only academic knowledge but also the development of empathy, self-awareness, and interpersonal skills. Students were encouraged to engage in reflective practices and discussions on emotions, fostering a greater understanding of their own mental processes and behaviors. The incorporation of emotional literacy into the curriculum allowed individuals to navigate their emotions effectively and develop coping strategies for stressors. This holistic approach to education laid the foundation for a healthy mind and emotional resilience, highlighting the importance of integrating emotional wellness into educational systems for the overall well-being of individuals.

EMOTIONAL LITERACY IN EARLY EDUCATION

Early education plays a crucial role in laying the foundation for emotional literacy in children. By providing a supportive and nurturing environment, educators can help young learners develop the skills necessary to understand and regulate their emotions effectively. Teaching children how to name their feelings, express themselves in healthy ways, and empathize with others not only promotes emotional well-being but also enhances their social interactions and overall academic performance. Research has shown that children who are emotionally literate tend to have higher levels of self-esteem, resilience, and mental health. Therefore, integrating emotional literacy into early education curriculum is essential for promoting healthy emotional development in children. By equipping students with the tools to navigate their emotions, educators can empower them to lead fulfilling and successful lives both in and out of the classroom.

INTEGRATING EMOTIONAL WELLNESS INTO HIGHER EDUCATION CURRICULA

Incorporating emotional wellness into higher education curricula is paramount in cultivating well-rounded and resilient individuals. By integrating discussions on emotional intelligence, stress management techniques, and mental health awareness into academic coursework, students are equipped with the necessary tools to navigate the challenges of academic and personal life effectively. Developing emotional intelligence not only improves interpersonal relationships but also enhances self-awareness and self-regulation, crucial skills for success in various professional settings. Moreover, incorporating mental health resources and support services into the curriculum helps destigmatize seeking help for psychological issues, promoting a culture of openness and self-care on campuses. By prioritizing emotional wellness in higher education curricula, universities can empower students to prioritize their mental health and overall well-being, ultimately leading to a more successful and fulfilling academic experience.

LIFELONG LEARNING AND EMOTIONAL HEALTH

Lifelong learning is a crucial component of maintaining emotional health. By continuously seeking out new knowledge and skills, individuals can stay engaged and stimulated, which can prevent feelings of stagnation or boredom that may lead to emotional distress. Additionally, learning new things can boost self-esteem and confidence, providing a sense of accomplishment and mastery that can improve overall well-being. Lifelong learning also encourages adaptability and resilience, skills that are essential in navigating life's challenges and setbacks. Moreover, the process of learning itself can be a source of enjoyment and fulfillment, bringing a sense of purpose and meaning to one's life. In conclusion, prioritizing lifelong learning can lead to enhanced emotional health by fostering growth, resilience, and a sense of fulfillment throughout the lifespan.

XIX. THE ARTS AND EMOTIONAL WELLNESS

In the realm of emotional wellness, the arts play a significant role in promoting mental health and overall well-being. Through various forms of artistic expression such as music, visual arts, literature, and performing arts, individuals can tap into their emotions, explore their inner thoughts, and find a sense of catharsis. The creative process involved in producing art allows individuals to channel their feelings in a constructive manner, leading to a deep sense of fulfillment and self-discovery. Moreover, engaging with art can serve as a form of therapy, providing individuals with a safe space to express themselves and cope with difficult emotions. Research has shown that participation in artistic activities can reduce stress, anxiety, and depression, ultimately contributing to improved emotional health. Therefore, incorporating the arts into one's daily routine can be a vital component of maintaining a healthy mind and emotional well-being.

EXPRESSIVE ARTS THERAPIES

The integration of expressive arts therapies into mental health treatment plans has gained recognition as a valuable tool for promoting emotional wellness. By engaging individuals in creative activities such as visual arts, music, dance, and drama, these therapies offer a non-verbal outlet for exploring and expressing emotions. Research shows that engaging in the arts can help individuals process difficult feelings, reduce stress, and increase self-awareness. Moreover, the artistic process itself can serve as a form of mindfulness, allowing individuals to be fully present in the moment and cultivate a sense of calm. As such, incorporating expressive arts therapies into mental health interventions can provide a holistic approach to emotional well-being, addressing the mind, body, and spirit. Overall, these therapies offer a unique and effective way to support individuals in their journey towards emotional healing and growth.

THE ROLE OF CREATIVITY IN EMOTIONAL EXPRESSION

Creativity plays a pivotal role in emotional expression, offering individuals a unique outlet to convey complex feelings. By engaging in creative activities such as painting, writing, or music, individuals can tap into their inner emotions and express them in a tangible form. This process enables individuals to explore their thoughts and feelings in a safe and controlled environment, fostering self-awareness and emotional intelligence. Moreover, creativity allows individuals to communicate their emotions in a non-verbal manner, transcending language barriers and cultural differences. Through the act of creation, individuals can find healing and catharsis, transforming their emotional turmoil into something beautiful and meaningful. Ultimately, creativity serves as a powerful tool for emotional expression, empowering individuals to connect with their inner selves and the world around them.

THE ARTS AS A TOOL FOR EMOTIONAL HEALING

The arts have long been recognized as a powerful tool for emotional healing, offering individuals a creative outlet to express and explore their innermost thoughts and feelings. Through mediums such as visual arts, music, dance, and writing, individuals can delve into their emotions, helping to process and release pent-up feelings of sadness, anger, or anxiety. Creative expression can also serve as a form of catharsis, allowing individuals to gain a sense of relief and release from emotional burdens. Moreover, engaging in artistic activities can promote mindfulness and self-awareness, fostering a deeper understanding of one's emotional state and facilitating personal growth. By integrating the arts into therapeutic interventions, individuals can harness the healing power of creativity to promote emotional well-being and cultivate a healthier mindset.

XX. NATURE AND EMOTIONAL HEALTH

Nature has been shown to have a profound impact on emotional health, with numerous studies highlighting the positive effects of spending time outdoors on well-being. The sights and sounds of nature can evoke a sense of calm and relaxation, reducing stress and anxiety levels. Moreover, exposure to natural environments has been linked to improved mood and cognitive function. This connection between nature and emotional well-being is rooted in the concept of biophilia, which suggests that humans have an innate affinity for the natural world. By immersing oneself in nature, individuals can reap the benefits of improved mental health and overall well-being. Therefore, incorporating regular outdoor activities or simply spending time in green spaces can be a practical and effective strategy for enhancing emotional wellness. As such, harnessing the power of nature may serve as a valuable tool in promoting and maintaining a healthy mind.

BIOPHILIA AND THE HUMAN CONNECTION TO NATURE

Biophilia, the innate human tendency to connect with nature, plays a crucial role in fostering emotional wellness. Research suggests that exposure to natural environments can improve mood, reduce stress, and enhance overall mental well-being. This connection to nature is deeply rooted in our evolutionary history, as humans have evolved in natural environments and have an inherent affinity for the natural world. In today's urbanized and technology-driven society, maintaining a strong connection to nature is vital for promoting emotional health. By immersing ourselves in natural settings, whether through outdoor activities or simply incorporating elements of nature into our daily lives, we can reap the benefits of biophilia and cultivate a sense of inner peace and harmony. Embracing our biophilic instincts can lead to a more balanced and fulfilling emotional life, ultimately contributing to a healthier mind and enhanced overall well-being.

ECOTHERAPY AND NATURE-BASED INTERVENTIONS

Ecotherapy and nature-based interventions have garnered attention in recent years for their potential to improve mental health and emotional well-being. By immersing individuals in natural environments, these therapeutic approaches aim to reconnect people with the natural world, providing a sense of peace and serenity that can be lacking in urbanized settings. Research has shown that exposure to nature can reduce stress, anxiety, and depression, while also enhancing mood and cognitive function. Moreover, engaging in activities such as gardening, hiking, or simply spending time outdoors has been linked to increased feelings of happiness and overall life satisfaction. Incorporating ecotherapy into traditional mental health practices offers a holistic approach to emotional wellness, encouraging individuals to find solace and healing in the beauty of the natural world. As society continues to grapple with high levels of stress and mental health issues, ecotherapy serves as a compelling and innovative intervention for promoting a healthy mind.

THE BENEFITS OF GREEN SPACES FOR EMOTIONAL WELLNESS

Green spaces have been shown to have a profound impact on emotional wellness, providing a range of benefits that contribute to overall mental health. In urban environments, where stress and anxiety levels can be high, the presence of green spaces offers a refuge for individuals to unwind and recharge. The calming effects of nature can help reduce feelings of tension and promote relaxation, ultimately leading to improved emotional well-being. Research has shown that spending time in green spaces can also enhance mood, increase self-esteem, and boost cognitive function. Furthermore, the social aspect of green spaces, such as community gardens or parks, can foster a sense of belonging and connectedness, which are essential for emotional resilience. Overall, the integration of green spaces into urban planning can significantly improve emotional wellness and contribute to a healthier, happier society.

XXI. SPIRITUALITY AND EMOTIONAL WELLNESS

Spirituality plays a crucial role in promoting emotional wellness, as it provides individuals with a sense of purpose, meaning, and connection to something greater than themselves. Through spiritual practices such as meditation, prayer, or mindfulness, individuals can cultivate inner peace, resilience, and gratitude, which are essential components of emotional well-being. Research has shown that individuals who engage in spiritual activities report lower levels of stress, anxiety, and depression, and have better overall mental health outcomes. Moreover, spiritual beliefs can help individuals cope with adversity, find strength in times of struggle, and experience a greater sense of hope and optimism. By nurturing their spiritual well-being, individuals can enhance their emotional wellness and experience a deeper sense of fulfillment and contentment in their lives. Ultimately, integrating spirituality into one's daily life can be a powerful tool for promoting emotional well-being and cultivating a healthy mind.

VARIOUS SPIRITUAL APPROACHES TO EMOTIONAL HEALTH

Various spiritual approaches to emotional health offer individuals different paths to achieve inner peace and balance. Mindfulness practices rooted in Buddhism encourage individuals to be present in the moment, acknowledging and accepting their emotions without judgment. This approach can help individuals develop a deeper understanding of their emotional patterns and triggers. On the other hand, practices such as prayer and meditation in Christianity can provide comfort and strength during times of distress, fostering a sense of connection to a higher power. Additionally, practices like yoga in Hinduism emphasize the importance of physical health in conjunction with mental and emotional well-being. By integrating these diverse spiritual approaches, individuals can cultivate a holistic approach to emotional health that addresses the interconnectedness of mind, body, and spirit, ultimately promoting overall wellness and resilience.

THE ROLE OF MEDITATION AND PRAYER

The role of meditation and prayer in fostering emotional wellness cannot be understated. Meditation offers a profound opportunity to cultivate mindfulness, awareness, and inner peace. By quieting the mind and focusing on the present moment, individuals can gain a deeper understanding of their thoughts and emotions. This self-awareness can lead to better emotional regulation and a greater sense of clarity. Additionally, prayer can provide solace and comfort in times of distress, offering a connection to something greater than oneself. Whether through traditional religious practices or personal spiritual beliefs, prayer can offer a sense of support and guidance. Combining meditation and prayer in a daily practice can enhance emotional resilience, promote a sense of inner balance, and lead to overall well-being. Ultimately, integrating these practices into our lives can contribute significantly to our emotional health and wellness.

THE IMPACT OF SPIRITUAL COMMUNITIES

The impact of spiritual communities on emotional wellness is profound and multifaceted. These communities provide individuals with a sense of belonging, purpose, and support, which are essential components of mental health. By coming together to practice and share their beliefs, members of spiritual communities can find solace in times of distress, guidance in moments of uncertainty, and a sense of connection to something larger than themselves. This communal support can help individuals navigate life's challenges more effectively and foster a sense of inner peace and resilience. Furthermore, participation in spiritual communities often includes practices such as mindfulness, meditation, and prayer, which have been shown to have significant mental health benefits. Overall, the impact of spiritual communities on emotional wellness is undeniable, making them a valuable resource in promoting holistic well-being.

XXII. SUBSTANCE USE AND EMOTIONAL HEALTH

Substance use and emotional health are intertwined in complex ways, often leading to a vicious cycle of dependency and mental health issues. Individuals struggling with emotional challenges may turn to substances as a coping mechanism, seeking temporary relief from their pain. However, this short-term solution can exacerbate underlying emotional issues and create long-term dependency issues. Conversely, chronic substance use can also impact emotional well-being by altering brain chemistry and leading to mood disturbances such as depression and anxiety. To effectively address both substance use and emotional health, a comprehensive approach that integrates mental health treatment and substance abuse interventions is necessary. By addressing the root causes of both issues concurrently, individuals can work towards achieving sustainable recovery and emotional well-being. This holistic approach acknowledges the interconnected nature of substance use and emotional health, emphasizing the importance of addressing both aspects for long-term healing and wellness.

THE EFFECTS OF ALCOHOL AND DRUGS ON EMOTIONAL WELL-BEING

The effects of alcohol and drugs on emotional well-being are profound and multifaceted. At the outset, substances such as alcohol and drugs can act as coping mechanisms for individuals experiencing emotional distress or mental health issues. This temporary relief may lead to a cycle of dependence, exacerbating underlying emotional struggles. Additionally, the use of these substances can disrupt the brain's natural chemical balance, leading to changes in mood regulation and cognitive function. Over time, persistent substance abuse can result in a range of emotional issues, including depression, anxiety, and personality disorders. It is crucial for individuals to recognize the detrimental impact of alcohol and drug use on emotional well-being and seek appropriate support and treatment. By addressing substance abuse and fostering healthier coping mechanisms, individuals can work towards achieving emotional well-being and overall mental wellness.

RECOVERY FROM SUBSTANCE ABUSE AND EMOTIONAL HEALING

Recovery from substance abuse and emotional healing is a complex and multifaceted process that requires comprehensive and holistic support. Initially, individuals need to detoxify their bodies from the harmful substances that have been negatively impacting their physical and mental health. This detoxification phase is crucial for clearing the body of toxins and allowing for a fresh start. Following detox, therapy and counseling play a pivotal role in addressing the emotional and psychological aspects of addiction. Cognitive-behavioral therapy and other evidence-based approaches can help individuals understand the root causes of their substance abuse and develop healthier coping mechanisms. Moreover, support groups and peer networks can provide a sense of community and understanding, fostering emotional healing through shared experiences and mutual support. Overall, recovery from substance abuse is a journey that requires dedication, perseverance, and a comprehensive approach to achieve lasting emotional wellness.

PREVENTING SUBSTANCE-RELATED EMOTIONAL DISORDERS

Preventing substance-related emotional disorders is a complex and multifaceted task that requires a comprehensive approach. To begin with, it is essential to address the underlying reasons why individuals turn to substances in the first place. This could involve tackling issues such as trauma, stress, or mental health disorders through therapy and counseling. Additionally, providing education and awareness about the risks of substance abuse and promoting healthy coping mechanisms can help individuals make more informed choices. Moreover, implementing policies and programs that restrict access to harmful substances and promote a supportive environment can also play a crucial role in prevention efforts. By taking a proactive and holistic approach, we can work towards reducing the prevalence of substance-related emotional disorders and promoting emotional wellness in our communities.

XXIII. THE ECONOMICS OF EMOTIONAL WELLNESS

The concept of emotional wellness extends beyond individual well-being to have broader economic implications. Research has shown that emotional health can impact productivity, job satisfaction, and overall job performance. Employers are becoming increasingly aware of the importance of supporting the emotional well-being of their employees, as it can lead to reduced absenteeism, lower turnover rates, and higher levels of job engagement. This shift in focus highlights the economic benefits of promoting emotional wellness in the workplace. By investing in programs that support mental health, companies can create a more positive and productive work environment, ultimately leading to improved financial outcomes. In today's competitive market, organizations that prioritize emotional wellness are likely to attract and retain top talent, enhancing their overall success and profitability. Therefore, it is clear that the economics of emotional wellness are a strategic investment for both individuals and businesses alike.

THE COST OF EMOTIONAL DISORDERS TO SOCIETY

Emotional disorders impose a significant economic burden on society, affecting individuals, families, workplaces, and healthcare systems. The cost of emotional disorders includes direct expenses related to treatment and care, as well as indirect costs stemming from reduced productivity, absenteeism, and disability. These disorders can lead to lost workdays, decreased job performance, and strained interpersonal relationships, further exacerbating the societal impact. Moreover, the healthcare system must bear the weight of providing appropriate services and support for individuals with emotional disorders, adding strain to already overburdened resources. As a result, addressing the cost of emotional disorders to society requires a multi-faceted approach that includes prevention, early intervention, and effective treatment strategies to alleviate the economic and social consequences. By investing in mental health resources and support systems, society can mitigate the far-reaching effects of emotional disorders and promote overall well-being.

INVESTMENT IN EMOTIONAL WELLNESS PROGRAMS

Investment in emotional wellness programs is crucial in promoting overall mental health and well-being. By providing individuals with the tools and resources to manage stress, anxiety, and other emotional challenges, these programs can significantly improve their quality of life. Research has shown that investing in emotional wellness programs can lead to a reduction in absenteeism, decreased healthcare costs, and increased productivity in the workplace. Moreover, supporting mental health initiatives can help create a more positive organizational culture, fostering a sense of community and support among employees. Ultimately, by prioritizing emotional wellness, organizations can create a healthier and more productive workforce, leading to long-term benefits for both employees and the organization as a whole. It is essential for organizations to recognize the importance of emotional well-being and make the necessary investments to support it.

ECONOMIC BARRIERS TO ACCESSING MENTAL HEALTH CARE

Accessing mental health care can be a significant challenge for individuals facing economic barriers. Low-income individuals often struggle to afford the costs associated with therapy sessions, medication, and other necessary treatments. This financial burden can deter individuals from seeking the help they need, leading to untreated mental health issues and potentially exacerbating the situation. Additionally, limited insurance coverage for mental health services further compounds the economic obstacles to accessing care. Those without adequate insurance may be forced to choose between paying for mental health services or other essential needs, creating a difficult decision that can impact their overall well-being. Addressing economic barriers to mental health care is crucial in ensuring that all individuals have equal access to the support they need for optimal emotional wellness. By implementing policies that reduce financial burdens and increase insurance coverage for mental health services, we can begin to break down these barriers and improve overall mental health outcomes for all individuals.

XXIV. LEGAL AND ETHICAL CONSIDERATIONS

In the realm of emotional wellness, legal and ethical considerations play a significant role in shaping the landscape of mental health support and treatment. As individuals navigate the complexities of seeking help for their emotional well-being, it is crucial to have a comprehensive understanding of the laws and regulations that safeguard their rights and privacy. Additionally, healthcare professionals must adhere to ethical guidelines to ensure the highest standards of care and respect for their clients. The intersection of legal and ethical considerations in mental health services underscores the importance of upholding confidentiality, informed consent, and the duty to report potential harm or abuse. By examining and adhering to these principles, both clients and providers can cultivate a safe and trusting environment that promotes healing and growth in the journey towards emotional wellness.

CONFIDENTIALITY AND PRIVACY IN EMOTIONAL WELLNESS SUPPORT

Confidentiality and privacy are essential components of providing emotional wellness support. Clients must feel secure in knowing that their personal information and thoughts are kept private, allowing them to freely express themselves without fear of judgment or breach of trust. By maintaining confidentiality, therapists can create a safe space for individuals to explore their emotions and work towards healing. Privacy in emotional wellness support also includes safeguarding electronic communication and data, ensuring that sensitive information is protected from unauthorized access. Respect for confidentiality builds a strong therapeutic alliance and enhances the effectiveness of interventions. Incorporating strict confidentiality protocols ensures that individuals can seek help without worrying about their privacy being compromised. In conclusion, confidentiality and privacy are fundamental in creating an environment conducive to emotional wellness support and promoting individuals' overall well-being.

ETHICAL DILEMMAS IN MENTAL HEALTH TREATMENT

The ethical dilemmas encountered in mental health treatment are complex and multifaceted, requiring careful consideration and ethical reflection by clinicians. One of the primary concerns in this field is the issue of informed consent, as individuals receiving mental health treatment may be in a vulnerable state and unable to fully comprehend the implications of their decisions. Additionally, maintaining confidentiality and privacy while balancing the need to protect the patient and others from harm poses a significant ethical challenge. Furthermore, the use of psychotropic medications and their potential side effects raise questions about autonomy and beneficence in treatment. These ethical considerations underscore the importance of a thoughtful and principled approach to mental health care, ensuring that the rights and well-being of patients are paramount in all decision-making processes. As mental health professionals navigate these complex ethical dilemmas, it is imperative that they prioritize the ethical principles of beneficence, non-maleficence, autonomy, and justice to provide compassionate and effective care for their patients.

LEGAL RIGHTS AND PROTECTIONS FOR THOSE WITH EMOTIONAL DISORDERS

Legal rights and protections for individuals with emotional disorders are crucial for ensuring their well-being and access to necessary support. At the heart of this issue is the concept of disability rights, as emotional disorders can significantly impact a person's ability to function in daily life. By recognizing emotional disorders as disabilities, individuals are entitled to legal protections under the Americans with Disabilities Act (ADA) and other relevant legislation. These rights may include accommodations in the workplace, access to mental health services, and protection against discrimination. However, there is still a gap in understanding and implementing these protections effectively. It is essential for policymakers, employers, and society as a whole to fully recognize and uphold the legal rights of those with emotional disorders to promote inclusivity and support their journey towards emotional wellness.

XXV. GLOBAL PERSPECTIVES ON EMOTIONAL WELLNESS

Global perspectives on emotional wellness are crucial in understanding the various cultural nuances and frameworks that shape individuals' mental health across the world. Different societies have unique ways of conceptualizing and managing emotions, influenced by factors such as religion, social norms, and historical experiences. For instance, Eastern cultures often emphasize the balance of yin and yang energies, promoting harmony and inner peace. In contrast, Western societies tend to prioritize individualism and self-expression as key components of emotional well-being. By exploring these diverse perspectives, we can enrich our understanding of emotional wellness and tailor interventions that are more culturally sensitive and effective. In an increasingly interconnected world, acknowledging and respecting global perspectives on emotional wellness is essential for promoting mental health on a global scale. By fostering cross-cultural dialogue and collaboration, we can work towards a more inclusive and comprehensive approach to emotional well-being.

EMOTIONAL HEALTH CHALLENGES IN DIFFERENT REGIONS

In examining emotional health challenges in different regions, it is crucial to consider the cultural and societal factors that influence mental well-being. This is particularly evident when comparing Western societies, where individualism is emphasized, to collectivist societies in parts of Asia and Africa. Western societies often prioritize self-expression and independence, which can lead to higher rates of anxiety and depression stemming from feelings of isolation and pressure to succeed. In contrast, collective societies place a greater emphasis on community and harmony, which may offer more social support but also bring about challenges related to conforming to societal norms and expectations. Understanding these nuances is essential in developing effective strategies for promoting emotional wellness on a global scale. By tailoring interventions to specific cultural contexts, mental health professionals can address the unique needs and challenges faced by individuals in different regions, ultimately fostering a more holistic approach to emotional well-being.

INTERNATIONAL INITIATIVES FOR MENTAL HEALTH PROMOTION

International initiatives for mental health promotion have gained significant traction in recent years, signaling a growing recognition of the importance of emotional well-being on a global scale. Beginning with collaborative efforts between nations to address mental health disparities, these initiatives have evolved to encompass a wide range of strategies, from advocating for policy changes to promoting mental health education and destigmatizing mental illnesses. These initiatives serve as a platform for sharing best practices, research findings, and resources to support the development of effective mental health promotion programs. By fostering international cooperation and dialogue, these initiatives aim to create a positive impact on the mental health of populations worldwide. As countries continue to face unique challenges in promoting mental health, international initiatives pave the way for a more holistic and comprehensive approach to addressing the complexities of emotional well-being in a global context.

LEARNING FROM GLOBAL APPROACHES TO EMOTIONAL WELLNESS

Drawing inspiration from global approaches to emotional wellness can offer valuable insights for promoting mental health on a broader scale. By examining various cultures' methodologies and practices for fostering emotional well-being, we can identify effective strategies that could be implemented in different contexts. For example, incorporating meditation techniques from Eastern philosophies or community-based support systems from indigenous cultures can enrich traditional Western approaches to mental health. This comparative analysis allows us to learn from diverse perspectives and adapt evidence-based practices to suit individual and community needs. Furthermore, by embracing a more inclusive and holistic view of emotional wellness, we can cultivate a deeper understanding of the interconnectedness between physical, mental, and spiritual health. Therefore, by studying and integrating global approaches to emotional wellness, we can enhance our existing knowledge and create more comprehensive strategies for promoting mental well-being worldwide.

XXVI. THE FUTURE OF EMOTIONAL WELLNESS

The future of emotional wellness, as articulated in XXVI, is poised for significant advancements driven by a deeper understanding of the complexities of human emotions and mental health. With the growing acceptance and prioritization of mental well-being, innovative approaches combining traditional therapies with emerging technologies are likely to shape the landscape of emotional wellness. Integrating artificial intelligence, virtual reality, and personalized digital tools into mental health practices could revolutionize the way individuals access and receive treatment, ultimately leading to more tailored and effective interventions. Moreover, the emphasis on preventive measures, such as mindfulness practices and emotional intelligence training, is expected to gain traction in promoting resilience and self-regulation. By harnessing the power of scientific progress and holistic approaches, the future of emotional wellness holds promise for more personalized and proactive strategies to nurture a healthy mind.

EMERGING TRENDS IN MENTAL HEALTH CARE

They have been shifting towards a more holistic approach that considers both the biological and psychosocial factors influencing mental well-being. This paradigm shift acknowledges the complex interplay between genetics, environment, and individual experiences in shaping mental health outcomes. As advancements in neuroscience continue to deepen our understanding of the brain, personalized treatment plans tailored to each individual's unique neurobiology are becoming increasingly common. Additionally, there is a growing emphasis on incorporating lifestyle interventions such as exercise, nutrition, and mindfulness practices into mental health care plans. Furthermore, telehealth services and digital mental health platforms have seen a surge in popularity, providing accessible and convenient options for individuals seeking support. These emerging trends signify a promising evolution in mental health care that prioritizes individualized, holistic approaches to promoting emotional well-being.

THE POTENTIAL OF PERSONALIZED MEDICINE

Personalized medicine holds immense potential in revolutionizing the healthcare landscape by tailoring treatment plans to individual patients based on their genetic makeup, lifestyle, and environmental factors. This approach allows for more targeted and effective interventions, minimizing adverse reactions and optimizing outcomes. By harnessing advancements in technologies such as genomics and bioinformatics, healthcare providers can offer precision medicine that goes beyond a one-size-fits-all approach. Additionally, personalized medicine fosters a shift towards proactive rather than reactive healthcare, emphasizing prevention and early detection of diseases. With the ability to predict risk factors and tailor interventions accordingly, personalized medicine has the potential to enhance patient outcomes, reduce healthcare costs, and improve overall population health. Embracing this model of care could lead to a more sustainable and efficient healthcare system, ultimately benefiting individuals and society as a whole.

PREDICTIONS FOR THE EVOLUTION OF EMOTIONAL WELLNESS PRACTICES

Predictions for the evolution of emotional wellness practices point towards a holistic approach that integrates traditional principles with modern scientific advancements. With the rise of technology and data analytics, personalized emotional wellness programs tailored to individual needs will become more prevalent. This shift towards personalized care will not only enhance the effectiveness of interventions but also improve the overall experience for individuals seeking emotional support. Furthermore, there is a growing emphasis on preventive measures, such as mindfulness practices and stress management techniques, to promote emotional well-being and resilience. As the field of emotional wellness continues to evolve, interdisciplinary collaborations between psychologists, neuroscientists, nutritionists, and mind-body practitioners will become more common, leading to innovative and comprehensive approaches to mental health. By embracing these advancements, the future of emotional wellness practices holds great potential in improving the quality of life for individuals across diverse populations.

XXVII. SELF-HELP AND PERSONAL DEVELOPMENT

The concept of self-help and personal development is a vital aspect of promoting emotional wellness. By focusing on self-improvement, individuals can enhance their self-awareness, set meaningful goals, and develop effective coping mechanisms to navigate life's challenges. Through practices like mindfulness, journaling, and self-reflection, individuals can cultivate a deeper understanding of their thoughts, emotions, and behaviors. This process of introspection not only fosters personal growth but also fosters resilience in the face of adversity. Furthermore, self-help resources and tools provide individuals with the necessary skills and techniques to manage stress, build self-confidence, and foster positive relationships. In essence, embracing self-help and personal development strategies is a proactive approach to cultivating a healthy mind and achieving emotional well-being.

THE ROLE OF SELF-HELP IN EMOTIONAL WELLNESS

Self-help plays a crucial role in promoting emotional wellness by empowering individuals to take control of their mental health. Through self-help practices such as mindfulness meditation, positive affirmations, and cognitive-behavioral techniques, individuals can develop coping skills to manage stress, anxiety, and depression. These practices foster a sense of self-awareness and mindfulness, allowing individuals to recognize and address their emotional needs effectively. Moreover, self-help tools provide a sense of autonomy and agency, empowering individuals to actively participate in their mental health journey. By incorporating self-help strategies into daily routines, individuals can cultivate resilience and improve emotional regulation. Ultimately, the integration of self-help practices can lead to a balanced and healthy mind, enhancing overall emotional wellness and quality of life.

EVALUATING THE QUALITY OF SELF-HELP RESOURCES

Evaluating the quality of self-help resources is crucial in maintaining the integrity and effectiveness of mental health interventions. The first step in this process is to assess the credibility of the source, ensuring that the information provided is evidence-based and supported by reputable research. It is also important to consider the qualifications and expertise of the author, as this can significantly impact the validity of the advice given. Furthermore, the clarity and accessibility of the material must be evaluated to ensure that it can be easily understood and implemented by individuals seeking support. By carefully scrutinizing these aspects of self-help resources, individuals can make informed decisions about which tools are most likely to benefit their mental health and well-being. In doing so, they can maximize the potential benefits of self-help interventions and contribute to their overall emotional wellness.

BALANCING SELF-HELP WITH PROFESSIONAL SUPPORT

Balancing self-help with professional support is essential in achieving optimal emotional wellness. While self-help strategies such as mindfulness meditation, exercise, and journaling can be valuable tools in managing stress and improving mental health, they may not always be sufficient on their own. Professional support, whether through therapy, counseling, or medication, can provide individuals with the necessary guidance and expertise to address deeper emotional issues and traumas. It is crucial to recognize when self-help methods are not yielding the desired results and to seek professional assistance when needed. By combining self-help practices with professional support, individuals can develop a comprehensive approach to emotional wellness that addresses both immediate concerns and underlying issues. This balance ensures that individuals receive the necessary support and resources to promote long-term emotional well-being.

XXVIII. THE POWER OF POSITIVE THINKING

The power of positive thinking is a crucial element in maintaining emotional wellness. Research has shown that individuals who adopt a positive mindset are more resilient in the face of challenges and tend to have better overall mental health. By focusing on positive thoughts and beliefs, individuals can reframe negative situations, reduce stress levels, and increase feelings of well-being. Embracing optimism can also lead to improved relationships, as individuals are more likely to approach others with compassion and understanding. It is important to note, however, that positive thinking does not mean ignoring or denying negative emotions; rather, it involves acknowledging difficult feelings while choosing to focus on the good in any given situation. Ultimately, cultivating a positive mindset can have profound effects on one's emotional and mental health, making it a valuable tool in promoting overall wellness.

UNDERSTANDING POSITIVE PSYCHOLOGY

Positive psychology is a branch of psychology that focuses on promoting well-being and happiness in individuals. By understanding positive psychology, individuals can learn to cultivate positive emotions, build resilience, and enhance their overall quality of life. Through practices such as gratitude journaling, mindfulness meditation, and acts of kindness, individuals can increase their happiness and satisfaction. Positive psychology emphasizes the importance of developing strengths and virtues to overcome challenges and achieve personal growth. By shifting the focus from pathology to a more holistic view of mental health, positive psychology offers a practical approach to emotional wellness. Ultimately, understanding positive psychology allows individuals to lead fulfilling lives by harnessing their inner strengths and positive emotions. By integrating the principles of positive psychology into daily practices, individuals can cultivate a healthy mind and promote overall well-being.

TECHNIQUES FOR FOSTERING OPTIMISM

Techniques for fostering optimism are crucial for enhancing emotional wellness. One effective approach is cognitive-behavioral therapy, which helps individuals identify and challenge negative thought patterns, replacing them with more constructive and positive beliefs. Additionally, practicing gratitude can shift focus away from difficulties and towards appreciation for one's blessings, promoting a more optimistic outlook. Engaging in mindfulness techniques, such as meditation and deep breathing exercises, can also help individuals stay present and reduce feelings of anxiety or pessimism. Furthermore, setting achievable goals and celebrating small wins along the way can boost self-esteem and confidence, contributing to a sense of optimism about the future. By incorporating these techniques into daily routines, individuals can cultivate a more positive mindset and navigate life's challenges with resilience and hope.

THE LIMITS OF POSITIVE THINKING

Positive thinking has long been promoted as a key element in achieving emotional wellness and overall success. However, it is essential to recognize the limits of positive thinking in maintaining a healthy mind. While a positive mindset can undoubtedly boost one's resilience and motivation, it is not a cure-all for all emotional challenges. Over-reliance on positive thinking can sometimes lead to denial of negative emotions and suppress authentic feelings, ultimately hindering genuine growth and self-awareness. It is important to acknowledge and process difficult emotions rather than simply trying to think them away. Embracing a balanced approach that incorporates both positive thinking and emotional honesty can lead to a more profound and lasting sense of well-being. By understanding the boundaries of positive thinking and integrating it into a broader emotional toolkit, individuals can cultivate true emotional wellness.

XXIX. OVERCOMING TRAUMA AND BUILDING RESILIENCE

Trauma can have a profound impact on an individual's life, often leading to long-lasting emotional and psychological challenges. However, it is possible to overcome trauma and build resilience through a combination of therapeutic interventions and self-care practices. By seeking support from mental health professionals, individuals can process their trauma in a safe and supportive environment, allowing them to reframe their experiences and develop healthier coping mechanisms. Additionally, practicing mindfulness, engaging in regular physical activity, and maintaining social connections can help individuals strengthen their resilience and foster emotional well-being. Ultimately, by actively addressing their trauma and actively working towards building resilience, individuals can empower themselves to navigate through life's challenges with greater strength and adaptability. The journey towards overcoming trauma and building resilience may be arduous, but it is a powerful process that can lead to profound personal growth and transformation.

THE PSYCHOLOGICAL IMPACT OF TRAUMA

The psychological impact of trauma is a complex and multifaceted topic that requires careful consideration and understanding. Traumatic experiences can have lasting effects on an individual's mental health, leading to issues such as post-traumatic stress disorder, depression, anxiety, and even substance abuse. The way in which trauma is processed and integrated into one's psyche can vary greatly from person to person, making it crucial to approach each case with empathy and sensitivity. It is essential to provide appropriate support and therapy for individuals who have experienced trauma, as untreated psychological wounds can fester and lead to long-term negative consequences. By addressing the psychological impact of trauma head-on and providing adequate resources and care, we can help individuals heal and move forward towards emotional wellness and resilience. It is imperative for mental health professionals to be well-equipped to address trauma in order to promote healing and well-being in those who have suffered.

THERAPEUTIC APPROACHES TO TRAUMA RECOVERY

Therapeutic approaches to trauma recovery play a fundamental role in promoting emotional wellness and healing. One effective method is CBT, which focuses on challenging and changing negative thought patterns and behaviors associated with trauma. Through CBT, individuals can learn coping strategies to manage distressing emotions and navigate triggers more effectively. Another valuable approach is Eye Movement Desensitization and Reprocessing (EMDR), which enables individuals to reprocess traumatic memories in a safe environment, ultimately reducing their emotional impact. Additionally, mindfulness-based interventions have shown promise in promoting self-awareness and emotional regulation, allowing individuals to develop a greater sense of control over their emotions. By integrating these therapeutic modalities, individuals can embark on a transformative journey towards healing and psychological well-being, leading to a healthier mind and a brighter future.

STRATEGIES FOR DEVELOPING RESILIENCE

In developing resilience, it is essential to employ a range of strategies that encompass physical, emotional, and cognitive aspects. Engaging in regular physical activity can serve as a foundation for building resilience, as exercise has been shown to enhance mood, reduce stress, and improve overall well-being. Cultivating emotional resilience involves developing self-awareness and acceptance of one's emotions, as well as practicing adaptive coping mechanisms such as mindfulness and positive self-talk. Additionally, fostering cognitive resilience entails challenging negative thought patterns, reframing setbacks as opportunities for growth, and cultivating a mindset of optimism and flexibility. By integrating these strategies into daily life, individuals can enhance their capacity to bounce back from adversity, cope effectively with stress, and maintain a sense of well-being in the face of challenges. Ultimately, a holistic approach to developing resilience can empower individuals to navigate life's ups and downs with greater ease and fortitude.

XXX. EMOTIONAL WELLNESS FOR SPECIAL POPULATIONS

Special populations, such as individuals with disabilities or chronic illnesses, often face unique challenges when it comes to emotional wellness. It is crucial for healthcare providers and support systems to understand the specific needs of these populations in order to provide effective mental health care. Tailored interventions, such as cognitive-behavioral therapy or mindfulness-based practices, can help individuals in special populations manage their emotions and improve their overall well-being. Additionally, creating a supportive environment that promotes positivity and empowerment is essential for fostering emotional wellness in these individuals. By recognizing the importance of emotional wellness for special populations and implementing targeted strategies, we can help them lead fulfilling lives and achieve optimal mental health outcomes. Collaborative efforts between healthcare professionals, caregivers, and community organizations are essential for promoting emotional wellness in special populations and ensuring they receive the support they need.

TAILORING APPROACHES FOR CHILDREN AND ADOLESCENTS

Tailoring approaches for children and adolescents is essential in promoting emotional wellness. Children and adolescents have unique developmental needs that require customized interventions to support their mental health. One approach is to consider age-appropriate coping skills and strategies that can be easily understood and implemented by young individuals. Additionally, taking into account factors such as cultural background, family dynamics, and individual strengths and challenges enhances the effectiveness of interventions. It is crucial to tailor therapeutic techniques to match the developmental stage and cognitive abilities of the child or adolescent, ensuring that the strategies are both beneficial and accessible. By personalizing approaches based on individual needs and circumstances, mental health professionals can better support the emotional well-being of children and adolescents, setting a strong foundation for lifelong mental wellness.

EMOTIONAL HEALTH CONSIDERATIONS FOR THE ELDERLY

Emotional health considerations for the elderly are paramount in ensuring a high quality of life as individuals age. It is essential to recognize that the mental and emotional well-being of older adults can be impacted by a myriad of factors, including social isolation, physical health challenges, and loss of independence. By addressing these factors proactively, we can promote resilience and emotional well-being in the aging population. Interventions such as cognitive-behavioral therapy, support groups, and mindfulness practices have shown promising results in improving emotional health outcomes for older adults. Additionally, promoting social connections, physical activity, and creative expression can help older adults maintain a sense of purpose and fulfillment in their later years. By prioritizing emotional health considerations for the elderly, we can support them in leading fulfilling and meaningful lives well into their golden years.

ADDRESSING THE NEEDS OF INDIVIDUALS WITH DISABILITIES

Addressing the needs of individuals with disabilities is a critical aspect of promoting emotional wellness for all members of society. By ensuring that individuals with disabilities have access to appropriate support services, accommodations, and resources, we can help them lead fulfilling and productive lives. This includes providing access to inclusive education, employment opportunities, healthcare services, and community support networks. It is essential to recognize that individuals with disabilities have diverse needs and abilities, and approaches to support must be tailored to meet these unique requirements. By promoting a culture of inclusivity and respect, we can create a more compassionate and understanding society that values the contributions of all its members. Ultimately, addressing the needs of individuals with disabilities is not only a matter of social justice but also a fundamental aspect of promoting emotional well-being for everyone.

XXXI. THE ROLE OF PHARMACOTHERAPY

The role of pharmacotherapy in promoting emotional wellness is a key component of modern mental health care. Pharmacotherapy, or the use of medications to treat mental health disorders, can often provide significant relief and support for individuals struggling with conditions such as depression, anxiety, or bipolar disorder. While therapy and lifestyle interventions play crucial roles in promoting emotional well-being, pharmacotherapy can offer a complementary approach that targets underlying neurochemical imbalances. It is essential to acknowledge the potential benefits of medication in addressing mental health issues, while also being mindful of the importance of proper diagnosis, monitoring, and adjustment of medication regimens. A holistic approach to emotional wellness should integrate pharmacotherapy with other forms of treatment to ensure comprehensive and personalized care for individuals seeking to achieve and maintain mental health.

MEDICATIONS USED IN TREATING EMOTIONAL DISORDERS

Medications play a crucial role in the treatment of various emotional disorders, providing relief to individuals who may struggle with symptoms such as anxiety, depression, or bipolar disorder. Beginning with an accurate diagnosis, healthcare providers can prescribe the appropriate medications tailored to each patient's unique needs. These medications work to balance brain chemicals and alleviate symptoms, promoting a sense of stability and well-being. However, it is essential to recognize that medications alone are not always sufficient in addressing emotional disorders. Often, a combination of medication and therapy yields the best results, as therapy can help individuals develop coping strategies and address underlying issues contributing to their symptoms. Therefore, a holistic approach that includes both medications and therapy is generally considered the most effective in treating emotional disorders and promoting long-term emotional wellness.

WEIGHING THE BENEFITS AND RISKS OF PHARMACOTHERAPY

Pharmacotherapy can offer immense benefits in the treatment of mental health disorders, providing relief from symptoms and improving overall quality of life. Medications such as antidepressants and antipsychotics have been instrumental in helping individuals manage conditions like depression, anxiety, and bipolar disorder. However, it is essential to weigh these benefits against potential risks. Adverse side effects, including weight gain, sexual dysfunction, and increased risk of suicidal thoughts, are common concerns associated with pharmacotherapy. Furthermore, the long-term effects of certain medications on the brain and body are not yet fully understood. Therefore, a thorough evaluation of the individual's specific needs, risks, and treatment goals should be conducted before starting any pharmacological intervention. While pharmacotherapy can be a valuable tool in promoting emotional wellness, it is crucial to consider the potential drawbacks and make informed decisions in collaboration with healthcare professionals.

THE IMPORTANCE OF MEDICATION MANAGEMENT

Medication management plays a crucial role in maintaining emotional wellness by ensuring individuals receive the appropriate treatment for their mental health conditions. Proper management of medications involves adhering to prescribed dosages and schedules, as well as monitoring for any potential side effects or interactions with other medications. Additionally, regular communication with healthcare providers is essential to discuss the effectiveness of the current regimen and make any necessary adjustments. Failure to manage medications properly can lead to treatment failure, exacerbation of symptoms, or adverse reactions. By taking a proactive approach to medication management, individuals can optimize the benefits of their treatment and improve their overall emotional well-being. Therefore, it is imperative for individuals to prioritize medication management as a fundamental aspect of their mental health care routine.

XXXII. ALTERNATIVE AND COMPLEMENTARY THERAPIES

Alternative and complementary therapies, such as acupuncture, aromatherapy, and mindfulness meditation, have gained popularity in recent years as individuals seek holistic approaches to enhance their emotional wellness. These therapies offer a different perspective on treating mental health issues and can complement traditional treatments. For example, mindfulness meditation can help individuals manage stress and anxiety by promoting relaxation and self-awareness. Acupuncture, on the other hand, is believed to balance the flow of energy in the body, leading to improved emotional well-being. Aromatherapy uses essential oils to stimulate the senses and create a sense of calm and relaxation. While these therapies may not be a substitute for medical treatment, they can be valuable tools in promoting emotional wellness. By incorporating alternative and complementary therapies into a comprehensive wellness plan, individuals can take a proactive approach to achieving and maintaining a healthy mind.

OVERVIEW OF ALTERNATIVE MEDICINE IN EMOTIONAL WELLNESS

Alternative medicine has gained popularity in recent years as a holistic approach to emotional wellness. This encompasses practices such as acupuncture, herbal therapies, yoga, meditation, and aromatherapy, among others. These alternative modalities are believed to address the mind-body connection, promoting overall well-being and emotional balance. Acupuncture, for example, targets specific points on the body to release blocked energy and restore balance. Herbal therapies utilize natural ingredients to support emotional health and reduce symptoms of anxiety and depression. Yoga and meditation help calm the mind and reduce stress, while aromatherapy uses essential oils to evoke relaxation and uplift the spirit. By incorporating these alternative practices into our wellness routines, we can enhance our emotional resilience and cultivate a healthy mind. This comprehensive approach recognizes the interconnectedness of our physical, emotional, and mental well-being, offering a more holistic and sustainable path to emotional wellness.

EFFICACY AND SAFETY OF COMPLEMENTARY THERAPIES

The efficacy and safety of complementary therapies have been a subject of debate in the medical community. While some argue that these therapies can provide valuable support for various health conditions, others are concerned about the lack of regulation and scientific evidence supporting their use. Proponents of complementary therapies point to their holistic approach, focusing on the mind-body connection and promoting overall well-being. However, critics raise valid concerns about potential risks and interactions with conventional treatments. It is essential for healthcare providers to approach the integration of complementary therapies with caution, thoroughly assessing each patient's individual needs and preferences. By conducting rigorous research and promoting open communication between patients and providers, the potential benefits of complementary therapies can be maximized while minimizing potential harm. It is crucial to strike a balance between embracing innovation and ensuring patient safety in the pursuit of holistic health and emotional wellness.

INTEGRATING ALTERNATIVE APPROACHES WITH CONVENTIONAL TREATMENTS

Integrating alternative approaches with conventional treatments in the realm of emotional wellness can offer a holistic and comprehensive approach to mental health. By combining traditional therapies such as cognitive-behavioral therapy with alternative practices like mindfulness meditation or acupuncture, individuals can address emotional issues from multiple angles, increasing the likelihood of successful outcomes. Alternative approaches can provide additional tools and strategies for managing stress, anxiety, and depression, complementing the effectiveness of conventional treatments. Moreover, incorporating alternative modalities into treatment plans can empower individuals to take an active role in their own healing process, promoting a sense of agency and control over their mental well-being. Overall, a synergistic approach that integrates various therapeutic modalities can lead to more personalized and effective interventions for individuals seeking emotional wellness.

XXXIII. PREVENTATIVE STRATEGIES IN EMOTIONAL WELLNESS

In the realm of emotional wellness, preventative strategies play a crucial role in maintaining mental health and happiness. One effective method is the practice of mindfulness, which involves staying present in the moment and being aware of one's thoughts and feelings. By cultivating mindfulness, individuals can recognize patterns of negative thinking or behaviors and address them proactively before they escalate into more significant issues. Another essential preventative strategy is building strong social connections and a support system. Having a network of trusted friends and family members can provide a sense of belonging and reduce feelings of isolation, ultimately contributing to overall emotional well-being. Additionally, engaging in regular physical exercise has been shown to boost mood and reduce symptoms of anxiety and depression. By incorporating these preventative strategies into daily life, individuals can take proactive steps towards maintaining a healthy and balanced mind.

EARLY INTERVENTION AND PREVENTION PROGRAMS

Early intervention and prevention programs play a crucial role in promoting emotional wellness and mental health. These programs aim to identify and address issues at the earliest stages, preventing them from escalating into more severe problems. By targeting individuals at risk or showing early signs of distress, these interventions can provide the necessary support and resources to prevent further decline in mental health. Moreover, early intervention programs equip individuals with coping strategies and skills to manage stress and build resilience, ultimately fostering emotional well-being. Research has shown that investing in prevention and early intervention programs can lead to long-term benefits, reducing the burden on healthcare systems and improving overall quality of life. Therefore, incorporating these programs into healthcare systems and communities is essential for promoting emotional wellness and preventing the onset of mental health disorders.

PROMOTING EMOTIONAL WELLNESS IN CHILDREN AND YOUTH

Promoting emotional wellness in children and youth is essential for their overall development and well-being. It is crucial to provide a supportive environment that encourages open communication and expression of emotions. In order to promote emotional wellness, adults must strive to create a safe and nurturing space where children feel comfortable sharing their thoughts and feelings. Teaching children healthy coping mechanisms and problem-solving skills can also help them manage stress and navigate challenging situations effectively. Additionally, promoting self-care practices such as mindfulness, exercise, and adequate sleep can contribute to a positive emotional state. By prioritizing emotional wellness in children and youth, we can empower them to build resilience, develop strong relationships, and thrive in all aspects of their lives. This proactive approach not only benefits the individual but also contributes to a healthier and more compassionate society as a whole.

COMMUNITY-BASED INITIATIVES FOR PREVENTION

Community-based initiatives for prevention play a crucial role in promoting emotional wellness within a society. By engaging with the community at various levels, these initiatives are able to address underlying issues that contribute to mental health concerns. These programs often focus on education, outreach, and support services that are tailored to the specific needs of the community. For instance, grassroots campaigns aimed at destigmatizing mental health issues can help individuals feel more comfortable seeking help when needed. Additionally, community organizations can provide a network of support and resources for those struggling with emotional challenges. By involving local leaders, healthcare professionals, and community members in the development and implementation of these initiatives, a sense of ownership and investment in mental health promotion is fostered. Overall, community-based efforts are essential in creating a sustainable and inclusive approach to emotional wellness.

XXXIV. CRISIS INTERVENTION AND EMERGENCY MANAGEMENT

Within the realm of crisis intervention and emergency management, it is essential to have a comprehensive plan in place to address situations that require immediate attention and care. When managing crises, it is crucial to have a well-trained team equipped to handle various emergencies, such as natural disasters, accidents, or mental health crises. This team should be able to assess the situation quickly, make timely decisions, and provide appropriate interventions to ensure the safety and well-being of all involved. Effective communication and coordination among team members are key elements in successfully managing emergencies and mitigating potential risks. Additionally, having clear protocols and procedures in place can streamline the response process and ensure that resources are utilized efficiently. By prioritizing crisis intervention and emergency management, organizations can effectively respond to unexpected events and minimize the impact on individuals and communities.

RECOGNIZING AND RESPONDING TO EMOTIONAL CRISES

Recognizing and responding to emotional crises is a crucial skill that individuals must develop to maintain emotional wellness. To effectively address emotional crises, it is essential to first understand the underlying causes and triggers that may lead to such challenging situations. By recognizing the signs and symptoms of an emotional crisis, individuals can take proactive measures to manage their emotions and seek appropriate support when needed. Moreover, responding to emotional crises requires a multifaceted approach that may involve reaching out to a mental health professional, engaging in self-care practices, and fostering supportive relationships. By acknowledging and addressing emotional crises in a timely and effective manner, individuals can enhance their overall emotional well-being and resilience. Ultimately, developing the ability to recognize and respond to emotional crises is a pivotal aspect of maintaining a healthy mind and achieving emotional wellness.

SUPPORT SYSTEMS FOR ACUTE EMOTIONAL DISTRESS

Support systems for acute emotional distress play a critical role in promoting emotional wellness. Beginning with the availability of crisis hotlines and helplines, individuals in distress can seek immediate support and guidance. These services offer a confidential space for individuals to express their emotions and receive valuable coping strategies. Additionally, professional counseling services provide a more structured and ongoing form of support for those experiencing acute emotional distress. By working with trained therapists, individuals can explore the root causes of their distress and develop personalized strategies for managing their emotions. Furthermore, peer support groups offer a sense of community and understanding, allowing individuals to connect with others who may be experiencing similar challenges. Overall, these support systems work together to address acute emotional distress in a comprehensive and holistic manner, promoting overall emotional wellness and resilience.

POST-CRISIS RECOVERY AND SUPPORT

In the aftermath of a crisis, individuals require a comprehensive approach to recovery and support to rebuild their emotional well-being. Post-crisis interventions should focus on providing immediate psychological first aid to address acute distress and stabilize emotions. This initial phase must be followed by ongoing mental health support, including counseling, therapy, and access to resources for long-term healing. Additionally, fostering resilience and coping mechanisms is crucial in helping individuals navigate the challenges that arise during the recovery process. Collaborative efforts between mental health professionals, community organizations, and support networks are essential in creating a holistic framework for post-crisis recovery. By addressing the multifaceted needs of individuals in a coordinated manner, we can promote emotional wellness and facilitate a successful journey towards healing and restoration.

XXXV. ADVOCACY AND AWARENESS CAMPAIGNS

Advocacy and awareness campaigns play a crucial role in promoting emotional wellness by raising public consciousness about mental health issues. These campaigns serve as platforms for sharing information, debunking misconceptions, and advocating for better support and resources for individuals struggling with emotional challenges. By bringing these issues to the forefront, advocacy campaigns aim to reduce stigma, increase access to mental health services, and foster a more supportive and understanding community. Through education and empowerment, these campaigns enable individuals to recognize the signs of emotional distress, seek help when needed, and support others in their journey towards emotional well-being. In a society where mental health is often overlooked or misunderstood, advocacy and awareness campaigns serve as catalysts for positive change, fostering a culture of empathy, understanding, and support for those navigating the complexities of emotional wellness.

RAISING PUBLIC AWARENESS ABOUT EMOTIONAL WELLNESS

Raising public awareness about emotional wellness is imperative in promoting individual and societal well-being. Initiatives aimed at educating the public about the importance of emotional health can lead to increased self-awareness, reduced stigmatization of mental health disorders, and improved access to mental health resources. By disseminating information through various channels such as workshops, seminars, social media campaigns, and community events, individuals can learn to recognize and manage their emotions effectively. Moreover, instilling a culture of openness and acceptance surrounding mental health issues can create a supportive environment where individuals feel comfortable seeking help when needed. Ultimately, by prioritizing emotional wellness and fostering a greater understanding of mental health, society can work towards breaking down barriers to care, enhancing overall emotional well-being, and promoting a healthier, more resilient population.

ADVOCACY FOR POLICY CHANGES AND FUNDING

Advocacy for policy changes and increased funding is essential in promoting emotional wellness on a societal level. By advocating for policies that prioritize mental health services and support, individuals can access the resources they need to maintain emotional balance and well-being. This includes advocating for increased funding for mental health programs, research, and education initiatives to address the growing need for mental health services. Policy changes can also help reduce the stigma surrounding mental health issues, making it easier for those struggling to seek help without fear of judgment or discrimination. By actively engaging in advocacy efforts, stakeholders can work towards creating a more supportive and inclusive environment for individuals with emotional wellness needs, ultimately leading to a healthier and more resilient society as a whole.

REDUCING STIGMA ASSOCIATED WITH EMOTIONAL DISORDERS

Reducing stigma associated with emotional disorders is essential for promoting emotional wellness among individuals. Stigma often leads to shame, fear, and avoidance of seeking help, creating barriers to accessing effective treatment and support. To address this issue, education and awareness campaigns are crucial in challenging misconceptions and promoting understanding of mental health conditions. Encouraging open conversations and providing accurate information about emotional disorders can help combat stigma and encourage individuals to seek help without fear of judgment. Additionally, promoting a culture of acceptance and compassion within communities can create a supportive environment for those struggling with emotional disorders. By reducing stigma and fostering an environment of understanding and support, we can create a healthier and more inclusive society where individuals feel empowered to prioritize their emotional well-being.

XXXVI. EMOTIONAL WELLNESS IN DIVERSE COMMUNITIES

Emotional wellness is a complex and multifaceted concept that is influenced by various factors, including cultural background, societal norms, and personal experiences. In diverse communities, the understanding and practice of emotional wellness can differ significantly, making it crucial to tailor interventions and support services to meet the unique needs of each group. By recognizing and respecting the cultural beliefs and practices of different communities, mental health professionals can create a more inclusive and effective approach to promoting emotional well-being. This approach requires sensitivity, empathy, and a deep understanding of the specific challenges and strengths within each community. By fostering a supportive and culturally competent environment, individuals from diverse backgrounds can feel empowered to seek help, address mental health issues, and ultimately improve their overall emotional wellness.

ADDRESSING DISPARITIES IN MENTAL HEALTH CARE

Addressing disparities in mental health care requires a multifaceted approach that acknowledges the complex interplay of biological, psychological, and social factors. The beginning of this process involves recognizing the existence of disparities in access to mental health services based on factors such as race, socioeconomic status, and geographic location. This acknowledgment must be followed by targeted interventions aimed at increasing access to care for marginalized communities. Middle interventions can include expanding mental health services in underserved areas, implementing culturally competent care practices, and addressing structural barriers to treatment, such as insurance coverage limitations. Finally, to ensure sustainability and long-term success, there must be a concerted effort to destigmatize mental illness and promote mental health education and awareness at both the individual and societal levels. By taking these steps, we can work towards a more equitable and effective mental health care system for all individuals.

CULTURALLY SENSITIVE APPROACHES TO TREATMENT

Culturally sensitive approaches to treatment are essential in addressing the diverse needs of individuals seeking emotional wellness. Beginning with an understanding of cultural background and beliefs, therapists can tailor interventions to resonate with the values and norms of their clients. This not only fosters a sense of trust and rapport but also ensures that treatment strategies are effective and meaningful. In the middle of the therapeutic process, it is crucial for therapists to continuously evaluate their approach and remain open to feedback from clients regarding the cultural relevance of interventions. This ongoing dialogue promotes a collaborative and empowering therapeutic relationship that honors the client's unique background. By the end of the treatment process, culturally sensitive approaches can lead to better outcomes, as clients feel understood, respected, and supported in their journey towards emotional wellness. Ultimately, integrating cultural sensitivity into treatment practices can enhance the overall effectiveness and impact of therapeutic interventions.

COMMUNITY ENGAGEMENT AND EMPOWERMENT

Community engagement and empowerment are crucial aspects of promoting emotional wellness. By actively involving individuals in their communities, they feel a sense of belonging and purpose, which can significantly impact their mental health. Empowering individuals to take ownership of their well-being through community initiatives can lead to increased self-esteem and a sense of control over their lives. Moreover, community engagement provides opportunities for social support and connection, which are essential for maintaining emotional stability. Through programs that encourage involvement in community activities and decision-making processes, individuals can develop a sense of agency and resilience in facing life's challenges. Ultimately, fostering community engagement and empowerment not only enhances individual well-being but also builds stronger, more cohesive communities that can collectively support and uplift each other in times of need.

XXXVII. THE ROLE OF PERSONAL RESPONSIBILITY

In exploring the notion of personal responsibility, it becomes evident that individuals play a crucial role in shaping their emotional wellness. Personal responsibility involves acknowledging one's actions, decisions, and behaviors, and taking ownership of the outcomes that result from them. This accountability empowers individuals to actively engage in self-reflection, self-improvement, and self-care practices that are vital for maintaining a healthy mind. By embracing personal responsibility, individuals demonstrate a commitment to their well-being and prioritize their mental health. This proactive approach allows individuals to cultivate resilience, cope effectively with challenges, and foster a positive mindset. Ultimately, the role of personal responsibility in emotional wellness highlights the significance of self-awareness, self-regulation, and self-empowerment in achieving a state of emotional balance and fulfillment. Embracing personal responsibility is not only a cornerstone of emotional resilience but also a fundamental aspect of personal growth and development.

ENCOURAGING PROACTIVE EMOTIONAL HEALTH MANAGEMENT

Encouraging proactive emotional health management is essential in today's fast-paced and stressful world. By taking a proactive approach to emotional well-being, individuals can develop the necessary skills and strategies to navigate challenges effectively. This can include practices such as mindfulness meditation, cognitive-behavioral therapy, and cultivating healthy coping mechanisms. Additionally, seeking professional help when needed and building a support system can also contribute to maintaining emotional wellness. By prioritizing emotional health and taking steps to manage it proactively, individuals can enhance their overall quality of life, improve relationships, and increase resilience in the face of adversity. Ultimately, investing in emotional well-being is an investment in one's overall health and happiness, making it a crucial aspect of holistic self-care practices.

SETTING PERSONAL BOUNDARIES FOR WELLNESS

Setting personal boundaries is essential for maintaining emotional wellness. By clearly defining what behaviors, actions, and attitudes are acceptable from others, individuals can protect their mental and emotional well-being. Establishing boundaries helps individuals prioritize self-care, communicate effectively, and avoid unnecessary stress and conflict. Consistently enforcing these boundaries reinforces self-respect and self-worth, which are foundational aspects of emotional wellness. Additionally, setting boundaries allows individuals to focus on their own needs and goals, fostering a sense of control and empowerment. This proactive approach to personal boundaries not only promotes a healthier relationship with oneself but also enhances interpersonal relationships by establishing mutual respect and understanding. Overall, recognizing and enforcing personal boundaries is a crucial aspect of emotional well-being and should be a central focus for anyone seeking to maintain a healthy mind.

ACCOUNTABILITY IN PERSONAL GROWTH AND DEVELOPMENT

Accountability in personal growth and development plays a crucial role in ensuring progress and success. Individuals must take ownership of their actions, choices, and behaviors to achieve sustainable growth and improve their emotional wellness. By holding oneself accountable, individuals can set clear goals, monitor their progress, and make necessary adjustments to stay on track. This process requires self-reflection, honesty, and a willingness to take responsibility for both successes and setbacks. Accountability also fosters a sense of empowerment and control over one's life, leading to increased self-esteem and motivation. Moreover, accountability promotes a growth mindset, where challenges are viewed as opportunities for learning and development rather than obstacles. Ultimately, by embracing accountability in personal growth, individuals can cultivate resilience, adaptability, and a positive mindset, contributing to their overall emotional well-being.

XXXVIII. THE IMPORTANCE OF ROUTINE AND STRUCTURE

In the realm of emotional wellness, routine and structure play a pivotal role in maintaining mental health and stability. The importance of routine and structure in our daily lives cannot be overstated. By establishing a consistent routine, individuals create a sense of predictability and organization, which can help reduce feelings of anxiety and stress. Moreover, routine offers a sense of control and empowerment, fostering a healthier mindset and greater resilience in facing life's challenges. Structure, on the other hand, provides a framework for tasks, goals, and responsibilities, ensuring that individuals can effectively manage their time and priorities. When routine and structure are incorporated into one's daily life, they can promote a sense of purpose, accomplishment, and overall well-being. Therefore, it is imperative to recognize and implement the benefits of routine and structure in cultivating a healthy mind.

ESTABLISHING DAILY ROUTINES FOR EMOTIONAL STABILITY

Establishing daily routines for emotional stability is essential in promoting overall well-being. Beginning each day with a structured routine can help individuals feel grounded and prepared to face any challenges that may arise. By incorporating activities such as meditation, exercise, and healthy meals into their daily schedule, individuals can cultivate a sense of balance and calmness. These routines can also provide a sense of predictability and control, which can be comforting in times of stress. In the middle of the day, taking short breaks to practice mindfulness or engage in hobbies can help maintain emotional equilibrium. Finally, winding down in the evening with relaxation techniques or journaling can promote a restful night's sleep, setting the stage for another day of emotional stability. Overall, establishing daily routines focused on emotional well-being can enhance resilience and improve overall mental health.

THE ROLE OF STRUCTURE IN MANAGING MOOD DISORDERS

Understanding the role of structure in managing mood disorders is crucial for promoting emotional wellness. Structured interventions, such as cognitive-behavioral therapy, provide individuals with the necessary tools to identify and challenge negative thought patterns that contribute to mood disturbances. By establishing a systematic approach to changing maladaptive behaviors and thoughts, individuals can gain a greater sense of control over their emotions. Moreover, structured routines, including regular exercise, healthy eating habits, and consistent sleep patterns, play a significant role in stabilizing mood and reducing the risk of mood disorder symptoms. Overall, a structured approach to managing mood disorders can help individuals develop healthier coping mechanisms, improve emotional regulation, and enhance overall well-being. Emphasizing the importance of structure in managing mood disorders can empower individuals to take proactive steps towards improving their mental health and achieving emotional balance.

FLEXIBILITY WITHIN ROUTINES FOR EMOTIONAL ADAPTABILITY

Flexibility within routines is essential for emotional adaptability. By incorporating elements of flexibility into our daily routines, we allow ourselves the opportunity to adjust to unforeseen challenges and changes. This adaptability promotes emotional resilience and helps us navigate through stressful situations with greater ease. However, it is important to strike a balance between structure and flexibility. While routines provide a sense of stability and security, being too rigid can hinder our ability to cope with unexpected events. By consciously incorporating flexibility into our routines, we can cultivate a mindset that is better equipped to handle the ups and downs of life. Ultimately, embracing flexibility within our daily habits can lead to improved emotional well-being and a healthier mindset overall.

XXXIX. EMOTIONAL WELLNESS AND AGING

Emotional wellness plays a crucial role in the aging process, impacting the overall quality of life for older adults. As individuals age, they often face a myriad of challenges that can have a significant impact on their emotional well-being. These challenges may include the loss of loved ones, declining physical health, and increased feelings of loneliness and isolation. It is essential for seniors to prioritize their emotional wellness by engaging in activities that promote positive mental health, such as regular exercise, social interactions, and mindfulness practices. By addressing their emotional needs, older adults can maintain a sense of purpose, resilience, and overall happiness as they navigate the aging process. As researchers continue to explore the connection between emotional wellness and aging, it is vital for healthcare providers and policymakers to consider the importance of supporting older adults in achieving emotional well-being as they age.

CHALLENGES OF EMOTIONAL HEALTH IN LATER LIFE

The challenges of emotional health in later life are multifaceted and often overlooked in discussions surrounding aging. As individuals grow older, they may face a myriad of stressors such as loss of loved ones, declining physical health, financial instability, and social isolation, all of which can take a toll on their emotional well-being. Coping mechanisms that once worked effectively in earlier stages of life may no longer suffice, leading to feelings of helplessness and despair. Moreover, the stigma surrounding mental health in older adults can prevent them from seeking the necessary support and treatment. It is imperative for healthcare providers, family members, and society as a whole to recognize and address the emotional needs of older individuals. By supporting their mental health and providing access to resources and therapy, we can help seniors navigate the challenges of aging with resilience and dignity.

STRATEGIES FOR MAINTAINING EMOTIONAL WELLNESS IN AGING

Strategies for maintaining emotional wellness in aging are crucial for overall well-being in the later stages of life. One approach is to prioritize self-care practices that promote relaxation and stress management, such as meditation, yoga, or mindfulness exercises. These activities not only help in reducing anxiety and depression but also enhance emotional resilience. In addition, maintaining social connections is another key strategy for emotional wellness in aging. Engaging in meaningful relationships with family and friends can provide a sense of belonging and support, reducing feelings of loneliness and isolation. Furthermore, staying physically active through regular exercise can have a positive impact on mental health by releasing endorphins and improving cognitive function. By adopting these strategies, older adults can effectively preserve their emotional well-being and enjoy a fulfilling quality of life.

SUPPORT SYSTEMS FOR THE ELDERLY

Support systems for the elderly play a crucial role in promoting emotional wellness and overall well-being in later stages of life. These systems encompass a wide range of services, including social support networks, community programs, and healthcare resources tailored to meet the unique needs of older individuals. At the heart of these support systems is the concept of social connectedness, which has been shown to improve mental health outcomes and decrease feelings of isolation among the elderly. Regular interactions with family, friends, and peers can provide a sense of belonging and purpose, combating the negative effects of loneliness and depression that often accompany aging. In addition to social connections, access to quality healthcare services and mental health professionals is essential for addressing age-related challenges and promoting emotional resilience. By fostering strong support systems for the elderly, we can help them navigate the complexities of aging with dignity and emotional stability.

XL. THE INTERSECTION OF PHYSICAL ILLNESS AND EMOTIONAL HEALTH

The intersection of physical illness and emotional health is a crucial aspect of overall well-being that is often overlooked in healthcare practice. The effects of physical illness on emotional health can be profound, leading to increased levels of stress, anxiety, and depression. Conversely, poor emotional health can also have a detrimental impact on physical health, exacerbating symptoms and prolonging recovery times. It is essential for healthcare providers to recognize and address this intricate relationship, considering the whole person rather than treating physical and emotional health separately. Integrated care approaches that incorporate mental health screenings, counseling services, and holistic treatments can help individuals manage both their physical and emotional well-being more effectively. By acknowledging the interconnectedness of physical illness and emotional health, healthcare professionals can provide more comprehensive and personalized care that addresses the unique needs of each individual.

EMOTIONAL RESPONSES TO CHRONIC ILLNESS

Emotional responses to chronic illness can vary greatly among individuals, yet there are common themes that emerge. At the onset of a chronic illness diagnosis, individuals often experience shock, denial, and a sense of loss. This initial reaction can give way to feelings of anger, frustration, and helplessness as the reality of the illness sets in. Coping mechanisms may vary, with some individuals turning to support groups or therapy while others may struggle in solitude. It is crucial for healthcare providers to acknowledge and address the emotional impact of chronic illness, as neglecting these aspects can hinder overall patient well-being. By fostering open communication and providing holistic care that encompasses both physical and emotional needs, healthcare providers can support patients in navigating the challenges of living with a chronic illness. Ultimately, understanding and addressing emotional responses to chronic illness is essential in promoting emotional wellness and overall quality of life for patients.

COPING WITH THE PSYCHOLOGICAL IMPACT OF PHYSICAL DISEASE

Dealing with the psychological impact of physical disease is a complex challenge that requires a multifaceted approach. The beginning of this process involves acknowledging and accepting the reality of the illness, which can be emotionally distressing for individuals. It is crucial for patients to engage in open communication with their healthcare providers, as this can help in gaining a deeper understanding of the disease and its implications. Additionally, seeking support from family, friends, or support groups can provide emotional comfort and guidance during difficult times. This middle stage involves actively participating in self-care activities, such as exercise, meditation, and relaxation techniques, to enhance emotional well-being. Finally, maintaining a positive outlook and resilience in the face of adversity is key to coping with the psychological aspects of physical illness. By following these strategies, individuals can better navigate the emotional challenges that come with managing a physical disease and strive to achieve overall emotional wellness.

INTEGRATING EMOTIONAL SUPPORT IN MEDICAL CARE

Integrating emotional support in medical care is paramount to holistic healthcare delivery. By recognizing and addressing the emotional needs of patients, healthcare providers can improve overall patient satisfaction, compliance with treatment plans, and health outcomes. This can be achieved through implementing strategies such as active listening, empathy, and building a trusting relationship with patients. Additionally, incorporating mental health screenings into routine medical visits can help identify underlying emotional issues that may be impacting physical health. By integrating emotional support into medical care, healthcare providers can offer a more comprehensive and personalized approach to patient care, ultimately leading to better overall wellness for individuals. Ultimately, by acknowledging the emotional aspects of healthcare, providers can create a more supportive and empathetic environment for their patients, fostering a more positive and effective healthcare experience.

XLI. EMOTIONAL WELLNESS IN TIMES OF CHANGE

In times of rapid change and uncertainty, emotional wellness becomes paramount for individuals to navigate challenges effectively. As old routines and structures are disrupted, it is natural for emotions such as anxiety, fear, and stress to surface. However, cultivating emotional resilience through self-awareness, mindfulness practices, and positive coping mechanisms can help individuals navigate these tumultuous times with grace and strength. By acknowledging and processing one's emotions, individuals can prevent them from escalating into overwhelming feelings that may hinder decision-making and problem-solving abilities. Furthermore, seeking support from loved ones, mental health professionals, or support groups can provide additional resources for maintaining emotional wellness during times of change. Ultimately, prioritizing emotional well-being is essential for individuals to adapt, grow, and thrive in the face of uncertainty and transition.

ADAPTING TO LIFE TRANSITIONS

Navigating life transitions can be a challenging process, requiring individuals to adapt and grow in response to changing circumstances. Whether it's transitioning to a new career, moving to a new city, or experiencing a shift in relationships, these changes can have a profound impact on one's emotional well-being. Adapting to life transitions involves recognizing and accepting the change, building resilience, and seeking support when needed. By acknowledging the emotions that arise during these transitions and actively working towards finding ways to cope, individuals can ultimately foster a sense of inner peace and stability. Developing healthy coping mechanisms, setting realistic goals, and maintaining a positive mindset are essential components of adapting to life transitions. Ultimately, embracing change as an opportunity for personal growth can lead to greater emotional wellness and overall life satisfaction.

THE EMOTIONAL IMPACT OF MAJOR LIFE EVENTS

Major life events such as marriage, divorce, job loss, or the death of a loved one can have a profound emotional impact on individuals. These events can trigger a wide range of emotions, from joy and excitement to sadness and grief. The way individuals navigate through these emotions can greatly impact their overall emotional well-being. It is important for individuals to acknowledge and process their feelings in a healthy way, whether it be through talking to a therapist, journaling, or seeking support from friends and family. By actively addressing and confronting their emotions, individuals can better cope with major life events and prevent long-term emotional distress. It is crucial for individuals to prioritize their emotional wellness and seek help when needed to ensure they are able to navigate through life's challenges in a healthy and effective manner.

STRATEGIES FOR MAINTAINING EMOTIONAL HEALTH DURING CHANGE

In times of change, such as transitioning careers or moving to a new city, it is vital to employ effective strategies to maintain emotional health. Firstly, cultivating a strong social support network can provide a sense of stability and comfort during periods of uncertainty. Surrounding oneself with friends, family, or support groups can offer encouragement, understanding, and perspective. Additionally, practicing self-care routines, such as exercise, meditation, or engaging in hobbies, can help manage stress and improve overall well-being. Setting realistic goals and boundaries for oneself can also foster a sense of control and accomplishment, reducing feelings of anxiety or overwhelm. Lastly, seeking professional help from a therapist or counselor can provide valuable guidance and support in navigating complex emotions and challenges. By implementing these strategies, individuals can effectively safeguard their emotional health and resilience during times of change.

XLII. THE ROLE OF LEADERSHIP IN PROMOTING EMOTIONAL WELLNESS

Effective leadership plays a crucial role in promoting emotional wellness within an organization. Leaders who prioritize the well-being of their team members create a positive work environment that fosters mental health. By implementing strategies such as open communication, active listening, and empathy, leaders can cultivate a supportive culture where individuals feel valued and understood. Moreover, strong leadership can help to reduce stress and prevent burnout among employees by promoting work-life balance and providing resources for mental health support. Leaders who lead by example in managing their own emotions and demonstrating resilience inspire their team members to do the same. In essence, the role of leadership in promoting emotional wellness is essential for creating a harmonious and productive workplace where individuals can thrive both professionally and personally.

LEADERSHIP QUALITIES THAT FOSTER EMOTIONAL HEALTH

Effective leadership qualities play a crucial role in fostering emotional health within individuals and organizations. Leaders who prioritize empathy, active listening, and open communication create a supportive and trust-based environment where emotional well-being thrives. Empathetic leaders are able to understand and connect with the emotions of their team members, leading to increased morale and a sense of belonging. Additionally, practicing active listening enables leaders to validate the feelings and perspectives of others, promoting a culture of openness and vulnerability. By encouraging transparent communication, leaders can address issues proactively, prevent misunderstandings, and build stronger relationships based on trust and authenticity. Ultimately, these leadership qualities not only contribute to emotional wellness but also enhance overall team performance and success. In an environment where emotions are acknowledged and supported, individuals can feel valued, understood, and motivated to achieve their full potential.

EMOTIONAL INTELLIGENCE IN LEADERSHIP

Emotional intelligence plays a crucial role in effective leadership, as it enables leaders to understand, manage, and express their own emotions, as well as empathize with the emotions of others. Leaders with high emotional intelligence can build strong relationships with their team members, manage conflicts effectively, and inspire trust and loyalty. By being able to regulate their own emotions, they can make rational decisions even in high-pressure situations, leading to better outcomes for their organization. Additionally, empathizing with team members allows leaders to understand their perspectives and motivations, enabling them to provide the necessary support and guidance. In today's complex and dynamic business environment, emotional intelligence has become a key competency for successful leadership, as it not only enhances interpersonal relationships but also fosters a positive organizational culture conducive to innovation and growth.

CREATING EMOTIONALLY HEALTHY WORK ENVIRONMENTS

Creating emotionally healthy work environments is essential for promoting overall well-being and productivity among employees. A starting point in this endeavor is fostering open communication and creating a culture where individuals feel comfortable expressing their thoughts and emotions. By promoting transparency and active listening, organizations can build trust and strengthen interpersonal relationships. Providing resources for stress management, mental health support, and work-life balance can also contribute to a positive work environment. Additionally, implementing wellness programs, mindfulness practices, and team-building activities can help cultivate a supportive and inclusive workplace. Ultimately, prioritizing emotional health in the workplace not only benefits individual employees but also has a ripple effect on organizational success and performance. As such, organizations must invest in creating an environment that nurtures emotional well-being to create a thriving and sustainable work environment.

XLIII. EMOTIONAL WELLNESS AND EDUCATION POLICY

Emotional wellness plays a crucial role in the development and success of students within the education system. As educational policies are crafted and implemented, it is imperative to consider the impact they may have on the emotional well-being of students. Policies that prioritize emotional wellness can lead to improved academic performance, increased student engagement, and overall better mental health outcomes. By incorporating strategies such as social-emotional learning programs, mental health resources, and supportive environments, educational institutions can create a nurturing and empowering space for students to thrive. Moreover, investing in emotional wellness within education policy not only benefits the individual student but also has broader societal implications, as emotionally healthy individuals are more likely to contribute positively to their communities and society at large. Thus, it is essential for education policy to prioritize emotional wellness in order to foster holistic development and success among students.

INCORPORATING EMOTIONAL WELLNESS INTO EDUCATIONAL POLICY

Incorporating emotional wellness into educational policy is crucial for promoting overall student well-being and academic success. Beginning with the importance of addressing mental health issues at an early age, educational policies should prioritize the development of emotional intelligence and coping mechanisms in students. By implementing programs that focus on mindfulness, emotional regulation, and stress management, schools can create a supportive environment that empowers students to navigate challenges effectively. Furthermore, integrating mental health education into the curriculum can help reduce the stigma surrounding mental health issues and promote a culture of openness and support. Ultimately, by prioritizing emotional wellness in educational policy, schools can not only enhance the academic performance of students but also foster a positive and healthy learning environment for all individuals involved.

THE BENEFITS OF EMOTIONALLY INTELLIGENT SCHOOLS

Emotionally intelligent schools offer a plethora of benefits for students, teachers, and the overall school community. By fostering a supportive and empathetic environment, these schools promote social and emotional skills that are crucial for success in both academic and personal realms. Students in emotionally intelligent schools are more likely to develop self-awareness, self-regulation, empathy, and effective communication skills. These skills not only contribute to better academic performance but also lead to improved mental health and overall well-being. Furthermore, emotionally intelligent schools help to create a positive and inclusive school culture, where students feel safe, connected, and engaged in their learning. Teachers in such environments are better equipped to cultivate strong relationships with their students and create a conducive learning atmosphere. Ultimately, the benefits of emotionally intelligent schools extend beyond the classroom, impacting students' future success and overall quality of life.

CASE STUDIES OF SUCCESSFUL POLICY IMPLEMENTATION

Case studies of successful policy implementation provide valuable insights into effective strategies for promoting emotional wellness at a societal level. By examining real-world examples of policies that have led to positive outcomes in mental health, policymakers can better understand what approaches are most likely to achieve success. One such case study is the implementation of school-based mental health programs in certain regions, which have been shown to reduce rates of anxiety and depression among students. This highlights the importance of early intervention and prevention initiatives in promoting emotional well-being. Additionally, analyzing the role of community partnerships in supporting mental health policies can provide guidance on how collaboration between various stakeholders can lead to more comprehensive and sustainable solutions. Overall, these case studies serve as powerful tools for guiding future policy decisions aimed at improving emotional wellness on a broader scale.

XLIV. THE MEDIA'S INFLUENCE ON EMOTIONAL WELLNESS

The influence of the media on emotional wellness is a topic that requires careful consideration, especially in today's digital age. The media plays a significant role in shaping our perceptions, beliefs, and attitudes, ultimately impacting our emotional well-being. From unrealistic beauty standards portrayed in advertisements to sensationalized news coverage causing anxiety and fear, the media has the power to either uplift or harm our mental health. It is crucial for individuals to be aware of the messages they consume and to critically analyze the content being presented to them. By developing media literacy skills and actively engaging with positive, empowering media, individuals can protect their emotional wellness and cultivate a healthier mindset. Ultimately, understanding and managing the influence of the media on our emotional well-being is essential for maintaining a balanced and resilient mental state in today's media-saturated world.

ANALYZING THE PORTRAYAL OF EMOTIONAL HEALTH IN MEDIA

The portrayal of emotional health in media plays a crucial role in shaping societal perceptions and attitudes towards mental well-being. Media often sensationalizes or stigmatizes mental health issues, perpetuating harmful stereotypes and misinformation. This can have detrimental effects on individuals struggling with emotional challenges, leading to increased stigma and barriers to seeking help. However, the media also has the power to destigmatize mental health by accurately portraying diverse experiences and promoting positive coping strategies. By highlighting stories of resilience, recovery, and empowerment, media can educate, inspire, and encourage open discussions about emotional well-being. It is essential for media professionals to approach the representation of emotional health with sensitivity, accuracy, and empathy, to contribute to a more compassionate and understanding society regarding mental health issues.

MEDIA LITERACY AND ITS ROLE IN EMOTIONAL WELLNESS

Media literacy plays a crucial role in promoting emotional wellness in individuals. By developing media literacy skills, individuals can critically analyze the information they consume, which in turn helps them make informed choices about the content they engage with. This ability to discern between accurate, unbiased information and manipulative or misleading content can contribute to reducing feelings of anxiety, stress, and overwhelm that often arise from exposure to sensationalized or inaccurate media portrayals. Moreover, media literacy empowers individuals to challenge harmful stereotypes, unrealistic beauty standards, and negative portrayals of mental health issues commonly found in mainstream media. By fostering a deeper understanding of how media influences emotions and behaviors, individuals can cultivate a more balanced and healthy relationship with media, ultimately enhancing their overall emotional well-being. As such, media literacy serves as a valuable tool in promoting mental health and emotional wellness in today's media-saturated society.

THE IMPACT OF SOCIAL MEDIA ON EMOTIONAL WELL-BEING

Social media has undeniably transformed the way we interact and connect with others, but its impact on emotional well-being is a topic of increasing concern. The constant exposure to curated and often idealized versions of others' lives on platforms like Instagram and Facebook can create feelings of inadequacy, envy, and lowered self-esteem. Research has shown a correlation between heavy social media use and increased feelings of anxiety, depression, and loneliness. Additionally, the constant need for validation through likes and comments can lead to a cycle of seeking external validation for one's self-worth. However, social media can also serve as a valuable tool for building connections, sharing experiences, and receiving support. It is crucial for individuals to be mindful of their usage and maintain a healthy balance to protect their emotional well-being in an increasingly digital age.

XLV. EMOTIONAL WELLNESS IN THE MILITARY

Within the military, emotional wellness plays a crucial role in the overall well-being and effectiveness of service members. It is imperative to recognize and address the unique stressors and challenges that individuals in the military face, such as deployment, separation from loved ones, and exposure to traumatic events. By prioritizing emotional wellness through access to mental health resources, training in coping strategies, and fostering a supportive environment, we can enhance resilience and decrease the risk of mental health issues among military personnel. Moreover, promoting emotional wellness not only benefits the individual but also strengthens unit cohesion and mission readiness. As such, it is essential for military leaders and healthcare providers to prioritize emotional wellness as an integral part of holistic care for service members, ultimately leading to a healthier and more resilient military force.

ADDRESSING THE UNIQUE EMOTIONAL CHALLENGES FACED BY MILITARY PERSONNEL

Military personnel face unique emotional challenges due to the nature of their work, including prolonged separations from loved ones, exposure to traumatic events, and the pressure to perform under high-stress situations. Addressing these challenges requires a comprehensive approach that combines mental health support, coping strategies, and resilience-building techniques. Providing access to therapy, counseling, and peer support groups can help service members navigate their emotions and develop healthy coping mechanisms. Additionally, promoting self-care practices, such as exercise, mindfulness, and creative outlets, can empower military personnel to prioritize their emotional well-being. By acknowledging and addressing the mental health needs of military personnel, we can better support their overall wellness and contribute to a more resilient and effective armed forces. It is essential to recognize and respond to the emotional challenges faced by military personnel to ensure their long-term mental health and readiness for duty.

PROGRAMS AND SUPPORT FOR VETERANS' EMOTIONAL HEALTH

When considering programs and support for veterans' emotional health, it is essential to prioritize comprehensive care that addresses the unique challenges faced by this population. Beginning with a holistic approach, it is crucial to offer a range of services that cater to the diverse needs of veterans, including mental health counseling, peer support groups, and access to specialized therapies such as cognitive-behavioral therapy and eye movement desensitization and reprocessing. Furthermore, creating a supportive environment where veterans feel safe and understood is paramount in fostering emotional well-being. This can be achieved through the establishment of veteran-specific support centers within communities, as well as partnerships with mental health professionals who have expertise in working with this population. By implementing tailored programs and support mechanisms, we can empower veterans to prioritize their emotional health and overall well-being, thus enhancing their quality of life post-service.

THE ROLE OF RESILIENCE TRAINING IN THE MILITARY

The role of resilience training in the military is crucial for enhancing the psychological well-being and combat readiness of service members. Beginning with a focus on stress management techniques, resilience training equips individuals with the skills to navigate challenging situations effectively. Through a combination of cognitive-behavioral therapy, mindfulness practices, and physical fitness, military personnel can develop the mental toughness needed to overcome adversity and thrive in high-pressure environments. By emphasizing coping strategies, emotional regulation, and social support networks, resilience training empowers soldiers to bounce back from traumatic experiences and maintain peak performance levels. In conclusion, the integration of resilience training into military education and training programs is essential for fostering a culture of mental toughness and emotional resilience among service members. Ultimately, investing in the psychological well-being of our military personnel is not only ethically imperative but also strategically advantageous for ensuring overall mission success and long-term operational effectiveness.

XLVI. EMOTIONAL WELLNESS AND THE JUSTICE SYSTEM

Emotional wellness is a crucial aspect that should be considered within the justice system, as it directly influences the mental health and decision-making processes of individuals involved. In the context of the justice system, emotional wellness can impact the behavior of both offenders and victims, influencing their ability to cope with trauma and navigate the legal process effectively. Research has shown that individuals with poor emotional wellness are more likely to engage in criminal behavior, highlighting the importance of addressing mental health within the justice system. By implementing programs that focus on improving emotional wellness, such as therapy and support services, the justice system can help individuals cope with the trauma they have experienced and reduce the likelihood of reoffending. Overall, prioritizing emotional wellness within the justice system can lead to better outcomes for both individuals and society as a whole.

MENTAL HEALTH CONSIDERATIONS IN CRIMINAL JUSTICE

A key aspect of the criminal justice system that often goes overlooked is the impact of mental health considerations on both offenders and the overall legal process. Research has shown that a substantial portion of individuals within the criminal justice system suffer from various mental health issues, ranging from depression and anxiety to more severe disorders like schizophrenia. These untreated mental health conditions can significantly impair an individual's ability to comprehend legal proceedings, make informed decisions, or adhere to conditions of probation or parole. Consequently, it is imperative for the criminal justice system to adopt a more holistic approach that incorporates mental health assessments, treatment options, and supportive services to address the underlying psychological factors contributing to criminal behavior. By recognizing and addressing the mental health needs of individuals involved in the criminal justice system, we can improve outcomes, promote rehabilitation, and ultimately create a more just and equitable society.

REHABILITATION AND EMOTIONAL WELLNESS PROGRAMS FOR OFFENDERS

Rehabilitation and emotional wellness programs play a crucial role in the successful reintegration of offenders into society. These programs aim to address the underlying issues that contribute to criminal behavior, such as substance abuse, mental health disorders, and lack of coping skills. By providing offenders with the necessary tools and support to address their emotional well-being, rehabilitation programs can help reduce the likelihood of recidivism. Through cognitive-behavioral therapy, mindfulness practices, and skills training, offenders can learn to manage their emotions, make better decisions, and build healthier relationships. Additionally, these programs can improve offenders' self-esteem and sense of purpose, leading to a more positive outlook on life. Overall, investing in rehabilitation and emotional wellness programs for offenders not only benefits the individual but also contributes to safer communities and a more just society.

SUPPORTING VICTIMS' EMOTIONAL RECOVERY

A crucial aspect of promoting emotional wellness is supporting victims in their emotional recovery process. Providing a safe and empathetic space for individuals to express and process their feelings is essential in helping them navigate the complexities of their emotions. This support can come in the form of counseling, therapy, support groups, or simply a listening ear from a trusted individual. Additionally, encouraging self-care practices such as mindfulness, meditation, exercise, and journaling can empower victims to take control of their emotional wellbeing. By offering these resources and tools, individuals can begin to heal from the trauma they have experienced and move towards a place of greater emotional stability and resilience. It is important to recognize the unique needs of each individual and tailor support to ensure that victims feel validated, heard, and understood as they work towards emotional recovery.

XLVII. INNOVATIONS IN EMOTIONAL WELLNESS RESEARCH

Recent advancements in emotional wellness research have shown promising results in improving individuals' mental health. Studies utilizing advanced technologies such as neuroimaging, wearable sensors, and big data analytics have enabled researchers to gain a deeper understanding of the complex interplay between emotions and mental well-being. These innovations have provided valuable insights into the neural mechanisms underlying emotional regulation and resilience, paving the way for more targeted interventions and personalized treatment approaches. By harnessing the power of these cutting-edge tools, researchers can identify biomarkers for various emotional disorders, develop innovative therapeutic techniques, and tailor interventions to individual needs. This paradigm shift towards a more data-driven and technology-enhanced approach holds immense potential for revolutionizing the field of emotional wellness research and ultimately improving the quality of mental health care for individuals worldwide. As we continue to embrace these innovative strategies, we are moving closer to a future where emotional well-being is optimized and mental health stigma is eradicated.

CUTTING-EDGE RESEARCH METHODOLOGIES

Cutting-edge research methodologies play a crucial role in advancing our understanding of emotional wellness. Utilizing innovative techniques such as neuroimaging, virtual reality, and big data analytics allows researchers to delve deeper into the complexities of the human mind. These methodologies offer unique insights into the neural pathways associated with emotional regulation, providing a more nuanced perspective on mental health disorders. By combining traditional research methods with these cutting-edge approaches, scientists can uncover new interventions and treatment strategies for individuals struggling with emotional well-being. Moreover, these advanced techniques enable researchers to explore the intricate interplay between biological, psychological, and environmental factors that contribute to emotional wellness. As we continue to push the boundaries of scientific inquiry, these methodologies will undoubtedly play a vital role in shaping the future of mental health research and practice.

RECENT FINDINGS IN EMOTIONAL HEALTH STUDIES

Recent findings in emotional health studies have shed light on the importance of addressing emotional well-being as a fundamental component of overall health. Research has shown that chronic stress can have a detrimental impact on both physical and mental health, emphasizing the need for effective strategies to manage emotions. Studies have also highlighted the role of positive emotions in promoting resilience and mitigating the effects of stress. Furthermore, recent research has underscored the importance of social connections and support in maintaining emotional health, pointing to the significance of building strong relationships and networks. By integrating these recent findings into holistic approaches to emotional wellness, individuals can cultivate a healthy mind and enhance their overall quality of life. This underscores the importance of prioritizing emotional health in promoting overall well-being and preventing the onset of mental health disorders.

THE FUTURE OF RESEARCH IN EMOTIONAL WELLNESS

The future of research in emotional wellness holds promising opportunities for advancing our understanding and treatment of mental health. As technology continues to evolve, researchers can utilize tools such as machine learning and data analytics to analyze large datasets and identify patterns in emotional well-being. This data-driven approach can lead to more personalized interventions and treatments tailored to individual needs, ultimately improving outcomes for those struggling with emotional disorders. Additionally, interdisciplinary collaboration between psychologists, neuroscientists, and medical professionals can further enhance our knowledge of emotional wellness and promote holistic approaches to mental health care. By combining cutting-edge technology with collaborative research efforts, we can pave the way for a future where emotional wellness is prioritized and supported in a comprehensive and effective manner.

XLVIII. THE ROLE OF NON-PROFIT ORGANIZATIONS

Non-profit organizations play a crucial role in promoting emotional wellness, particularly through their focus on community outreach and support services. These organizations often fill the gaps left by government agencies and provide valuable resources for individuals in need of mental health assistance. By offering counseling, support groups, and education programs, non-profits help individuals navigate their emotional challenges and develop coping mechanisms. Furthermore, these organizations advocate for policy changes and raise awareness about mental health issues, contributing to destigmatizing mental illness. Through their tireless efforts, non-profits create a more compassionate and supportive society for individuals struggling with emotional wellness. In essence, their dedication to promoting mental health positively impacts individuals, families, and communities, making them essential partners in the journey towards emotional well-being. By recognizing and supporting the important role of non-profit organizations, we can collectively strive towards a healthier, more empathetic society.

NON-PROFITS DEDICATED TO EMOTIONAL WELLNESS

Non-profits dedicated to emotional wellness play a crucial role in addressing mental health issues and promoting overall well-being in society. These organizations often provide essential services such as counseling, support groups, and educational programs to help individuals cope with stress, anxiety, depression, and other mental health challenges. By offering these resources free of charge or at low cost, non-profits make mental health support accessible to individuals who may not otherwise be able to afford it. Additionally, these organizations raise awareness about mental health issues and reduce stigma surrounding seeking help for emotional concerns. Through their efforts, non-profits not only support individuals in crisis but also work to create a more compassionate and understanding community where emotional wellness is prioritized. As such, the work of non-profits dedicated to emotional wellness is invaluable in promoting mental well-being on a societal level.

COLLABORATIONS BETWEEN NON-PROFITS AND HEALTHCARE PROVIDERS

Collaborations between non-profits and healthcare providers are essential for promoting emotional wellness on a larger scale. Non-profit organizations bring a wealth of experience in community outreach and advocacy, while healthcare providers offer clinical expertise and resources. By working together, they can create comprehensive programs that address the diverse needs of individuals struggling with mental health issues. These collaborations can bridge gaps in access to care, providing vital support and services to underserved populations. Additionally, partnerships between non-profits and healthcare providers can lead to innovative approaches to mental health treatment and prevention. Through shared knowledge and resources, these collaborations have the potential to make a significant impact on improving emotional wellness outcomes for individuals in need. Overall, these partnerships are crucial for creating a more holistic and effective approach to promoting emotional wellness in our communities.

THE IMPACT OF NON-PROFIT WORK ON COMMUNITY HEALTH

The impact of non-profit work on community health is profound and multifaceted. Non-profit organizations play a crucial role in addressing various health disparities and promoting wellness within communities. By providing access to essential healthcare services, advocating for health policies that benefit marginalized populations, and implementing preventative measures, non-profits contribute significantly to improving overall community health outcomes. Furthermore, these organizations often engage in health education initiatives, empowering individuals with the knowledge and resources to make informed decisions regarding their well-being. Through collaborative efforts with healthcare providers, government agencies, and community stakeholders, non-profits foster a holistic approach to health that prioritizes the unique needs of each community. Ultimately, the dedication and impact of non-profit work on community health are undeniable, creating a ripple effect of positive change for individuals and society as a whole.

XLIX. PERSONAL NARRATIVES AND CASE STUDIES

Personal narratives and case studies play a crucial role in understanding the complexities of emotional wellness. By delving into individual stories and experiences, researchers can gain valuable insights into the impact of various factors on mental health. These narratives provide a unique perspective that goes beyond statistical data, offering a deep and nuanced understanding of the human experience. Case studies, on the other hand, allow researchers to explore specific instances in detail, identifying patterns and potential solutions for improving emotional well-being. Together, personal narratives and case studies contribute significantly to the field of psychology, shedding light on the diverse ways in which individuals navigate challenges and find resilience. By incorporating these qualitative methods into research, we can enhance our understanding of the human mind and promote more effective interventions for emotional well-being.

THE POWER OF STORYTELLING IN EMOTIONAL HEALING

Storytelling has long been recognized as a powerful tool for emotional healing. Through the process of sharing personal narratives and experiences, individuals can gain insight, process complex emotions, and find a sense of connection and catharsis. The act of storytelling allows individuals to externalize their inner struggles and transform them into cohesive, meaningful narratives. By giving voice to their experiences, individuals can reframe and make sense of their past traumas, enabling them to move forward with a renewed sense of empowerment and resilience. Furthermore, through the act of listening to the stories of others, individuals can cultivate empathy, understanding, and a greater sense of community. In this way, storytelling serves as a bridge for healing, promoting emotional well-being and fostering a sense of shared humanity among individuals facing similar challenges.

ANALYZING CASE STUDIES FOR EDUCATIONAL PURPOSES

Analyzing case studies for educational purposes is a valuable tool in the realm of emotional wellness. By delving into real-life scenarios, students are able to apply theoretical knowledge to practical situations, enhancing their critical thinking and problem-solving skills. Case studies provide a platform for learners to explore different perspectives, understand the complexity of human emotions, and develop empathy towards others. Through in-depth analysis of cases, individuals can evaluate the effectiveness of various interventions, strategies, and approaches in addressing emotional issues. Moreover, case studies offer a holistic view of the interconnectedness of emotions, behaviors, and cognition, allowing for a more comprehensive understanding of emotional well-being. Ultimately, studying case studies in an educational setting fosters a deeper appreciation for the nuances of emotional wellness and equips individuals with the tools to navigate complex emotional challenges in their personal and professional lives.

ETHICAL CONSIDERATIONS IN SHARING PERSONAL NARRATIVES

Ethical considerations in sharing personal narratives are of utmost importance, especially in the context of promoting emotional wellness. Beginning with the understanding that personal narratives can be powerful tools for healing and connection, it is crucial to acknowledge the potential impact of sharing such intimate details. Middle The ethical dilemma arises when considering issues of consent, privacy, and potential harm that sharing personal narratives can entail. While individuals may find solace in sharing their stories, there is a responsibility to protect the privacy and autonomy of those involved. Therefore, careful consideration must be given to the potential consequences of sharing personal narratives, including the possibility of retraumatizing individuals or causing harm. End Ultimately, in navigating the ethical considerations of sharing personal narratives, it is essential to prioritize respect, consent, and sensitivity in order to uphold the ethical principles of emotional wellness and mutual respect.

L. SYNTHESIS OF KEY CONCEPTS

In the synthesis of key concepts pertaining to emotional wellness, it is essential to consider the interconnected nature of mental and physical well-being. Understanding the impact of lifestyle choices, stress management, and coping mechanisms on overall emotional health is crucial in fostering a healthy mind. By exploring theories of cognitive behavioral therapy, mindfulness practices, and the role of social support networks, individuals can develop strategies to enhance their emotional wellness. Moreover, acknowledging the significance of self-awareness, emotional intelligence, and resilience in navigating life's challenges is integral to maintaining a positive mindset. By integrating these key concepts into daily routines and prioritizing self-care, individuals can cultivate a balanced and resilient emotional state. Ultimately, the synthesis of these concepts serves as a guide for achieving optimal emotional wellness and building a foundation for long-term mental health.

INTEGRATING THE PRINCIPLES OF EMOTIONAL WELLNESS

Integrating the principles of emotional wellness is essential in establishing a healthy mind. Beginning with self-awareness, individuals must recognize their emotional states, triggers, and coping mechanisms. Through this introspection, one can develop effective strategies for regulating emotions and maintaining mental well-being. The middle section of this process involves cultivating emotional intelligence, which includes skills such as empathy, social awareness, and conflict resolution. These competencies enable individuals to navigate complex interpersonal dynamics and manage stress effectively. Finally, integrating emotional wellness principles into daily routines and decision-making practices ensures long-term mental health benefits. By prioritizing emotional well-being and consistently applying these principles, individuals can enhance their overall quality of life and achieve a greater sense of fulfillment and resilience in the face of challenges.

THE HOLISTIC APPROACH TO EMOTIONAL HEALTH

The holistic approach to emotional health encompasses the interconnectedness of mind, body, and spirit in achieving overall well-being. By recognizing that emotional health is not isolated from physical or spiritual health, individuals can address underlying issues that may be impacting their emotional state. This comprehensive approach considers how lifestyle factors, such as exercise, nutrition, and stress management, can influence one's emotional well-being. Furthermore, practices such as mindfulness, meditation, and therapy can help individuals develop self-awareness, regulate emotions, and cultivate resilience in the face of challenges. Embracing a holistic approach to emotional health encourages individuals to take proactive steps in caring for their mental and emotional well-being, leading to improved quality of life and increased resilience in navigating life's complexities. It underscores the importance of addressing emotional health as an integral part of overall wellness, promoting balance and harmony in all aspects of life.

SUMMARY OF BEST PRACTICES FOR MAINTAINING EMOTIONAL WELLNESS

In conclusion, maintaining emotional wellness requires a multi-faceted approach that incorporates various best practices. Firstly, engaging in regular physical activity has proven to be beneficial in reducing stress and promoting overall mental well-being. Additionally, developing strong social connections and fostering supportive relationships can provide a sense of belonging and a source of emotional support during challenging times. Practicing mindfulness and relaxation techniques such as meditation, deep breathing, or yoga can help individuals manage their emotions and reduce anxiety. Setting boundaries, prioritizing self-care, and seeking professional help when needed are also crucial components of maintaining emotional wellness. By incorporating these best practices into one's daily routine, individuals can cultivate a healthy mind and enhance their overall quality of life. It is important to recognize that emotional wellness is a continuous journey that requires ongoing effort and commitment.

LI. CONCLUSION

In conclusion, emotional wellness is a critical aspect of overall well-being, and nurturing a healthy mind is essential for a fulfilling life. By prioritizing self-care practices, such as mindfulness, stress management, and seeking support when needed, individuals can cultivate resilience and emotional balance. Developing a strong sense of self-awareness and emotional intelligence can lead to better interactions with others and a deeper understanding of one's own emotions. Additionally, practicing gratitude and positive thinking can shift perspectives and promote a more optimistic outlook on life. Ultimately, maintaining a healthy mind requires dedication, self-reflection, and a willingness to prioritize mental health. As we strive to navigate the complexities of modern life, it is crucial to remember that emotional wellness is a continuous journey that requires ongoing effort and commitment. By implementing the strategies outlined in this guide, individuals can take proactive steps towards achieving emotional well-being and living a more fulfilling life.

RECAPITULATION OF THE MAIN ARGUMENTS AND EVIDENCE

In conclusion, the main arguments and evidence discussed in this essay provide a comprehensive guide to achieving emotional wellness and a healthy mind. By emphasizing the importance of self-care practices such as mindfulness, stress management techniques, and seeking professional help when needed, individuals can work towards improving their overall well-being. The research presented delves into the psychological benefits of practicing gratitude, cultivating positive relationships, and engaging in activities that promote mental health. Additionally, the exploration of the mind-body connection highlights the importance of physical health in maintaining emotional balance. Overall, the amalgamation of these arguments and evidence paints a clear picture of the steps individuals can take to foster a healthy mind and emotional wellness in their daily lives. The practical tips and strategies outlined in this essay serve as a roadmap for readers seeking to prioritize their mental health and lead fulfilling lives.

THE IMPORTANCE OF CONTINUED RESEARCH AND PRACTICE

Continued research and practice in the field of emotional wellness is crucial for advancing our understanding and improving interventions for mental health. Through ongoing research, new discoveries can be made, leading to innovative treatment options and improved outcomes for individuals struggling with emotional difficulties. Practice, on the other hand, allows professionals to refine their skills and techniques, ultimately enhancing the quality of care they provide to their clients. Without a commitment to both research and practice, we risk stagnation in the field, hindering progress and limiting the efficacy of available interventions. By prioritizing continued research and practice, we can better address the complex and diverse needs of individuals seeking emotional well-being, ultimately leading to a healthier society overall. It is imperative that professionals in the field remain dedicated to advancing their knowledge and skills through ongoing engagement in research and practice.

FINAL THOUGHTS ON ACHIEVING AND SUSTAINING EMOTIONAL WELLNESS

In conclusion, achieving and sustaining emotional wellness requires a multifaceted approach that encompasses various aspects of one's life. It is essential to prioritize self-care practices such as regular exercise, proper nutrition, adequate sleep, and stress management techniques. Cultivating strong social connections and engaging in meaningful relationships can also contribute significantly to emotional well-being. Additionally, incorporating mindfulness practices, such as meditation and deep breathing exercises, can help individuals better cope with challenging emotions and situations. Seeking professional help when needed and being proactive about addressing mental health issues is vital for long-term emotional wellness. By taking a proactive and holistic approach to emotional well-being, individuals can cultivate resilience and effectively navigate the ups and downs of life with greater ease and stability.

BIBLIOGRAPHY

J. Rick Turner. 'Encyclopedia of Behavioral Medicine.' Marc D. Gellman, Springer New York, 1/1/2019

William C. Orr. 'Understanding Sleep.' The Evaluation and Treatment of Sleep Disorders, Mark R. Pressman, American Psychological Association, 1/1/2000

Guy C. Le Masurier. 'Fitness for Life.' Charles B. Corbin, Human Kinetics, 3/25/2014

Food and Nutrition Board. 'Front-of-Package Nutrition Rating Systems and Symbols.' Promoting Healthier Choices, Institute of Medicine, National Academies Press, 1/30/2012

David B. Allison. 'Obesity and Mental Disorders.' Susan L. McElroy, CRC Press, 1/13/2006

Andy P. Field. 'Anxiety Disorders in Children and Adolescents.' Wendy K. Silverman, Cambridge University Press, 8/25/2011

Todd J. Farchione. 'Unified Protocol for Transdiagnostic Treatment of Emotional Disorders.' Therapist Guide, David H. Barlow, Oxford University Press, 12/14/2010

Judith S. Beck. 'Cognitive Behavior Therapy, Second Edition.' Basics and Beyond, Guilford Press, 8/18/2011

Diane Shea. 'Cognitive Behavioral Approaches for Counselors.' SAGE Publications, 12/31/2014

Subhashni D. Singh Joy. 'Mindfulness-based Interventions with Children and Adolescents.' Research and Practice, Nirbhay N. Singh, Routledge, 12/13/2020

Patricia C. Broderick. 'Learning to Breathe.' A Mindfulness Curriculum for Adolescents to Cultivate Emotion Regulation, Attention, and Performance, New Harbinger Publications, 6/1/2021

Christina Feldman. 'Principles of Meditation.' Thorsons, 12/1/1997

Ed Halliwell. 'Mindfulness-- Report 2010.' Mental Health Foundation, 1/1/2010

Morrie Goldfischer. 'Why Me?.' Coping with Grief, Loss, and Change, Pesach Krauss, Bantam Books, 1/1/1990

Adam Grant. 'Option B.' Facing Adversity, Building Resilience, and Finding Joy, Sheryl Sandberg, Knopf Doubleday Publishing Group, 4/24/2017

Norman S. Endler. 'Handbook of Coping.' Theory, Research, Applications, Moshe Zeidner, John Wiley & Sons, 12/12/1995

Nicholas Weber. 'Easy Coping Strategies for Stress.' Discover Ways and Mechanisms to Reduce Stress for the Anxious Mind, Maclaxy Publishing, 1/1/2019

Institute of Leadership & Management. 'Managing Stress in the Workplace.' Routledge, 5/14/2010

B Hiriyappa. 'Stress Management.' Leading To Success, Booktango, 10/8/2013

Mary Wingo. 'The Impact of the Human Stress Response.' The Biologic Origins of Human Stress (a Practical Stress Management Book about the Mind Body Connection of Stress), Roxwell Waterhouse, 6/1/2016

Elizabeth P. Hayden. 'The Oxford Handbook of Stress and Mental Health.' Kate L. Harkness, Oxford University Press, 12/17/2019

William H. Coryell. 'Clinical Guide to Depression and Bipolar Disorder.' Findings From the Collaborative Depression Study, Martin B. Keller, American Psychiatric Pub, 4/10/2013

American Psychiatric Association. 'Diagnostic and Statistical Manual of Mental Disorders (DSM-5).' Booksmith Publishing LLC, 9/24/2021

National Collaborating Centre for Mental Health (Great Britain). 'Common Mental Health Disorders.' Identification and Pathways to Care, RCPsych Publications, 1/1/2011

Barbara Probst. 'Critical Thinking in Clinical Assessment and Diagnosis.' Springer, 4/30/2015

Bena Kallick. 'Assessment Strategies for Self-Directed Learning.' Arthur L. Costa, Corwin Press, 1/1/2004

Management Association, Information Resources. 'Learning and Performance Assessment: Concepts, Methodologies, Tools, and Applications.' Concepts, Methodologies, Tools, and Applications, IGI Global, 10/11/2019

Yvonne Stolk. 'Assessing Mental Health Across Cultures.' Lena Andary, Australian Academic Press, 1/1/2003

Food and Nutrition Board. 'Educating the Student Body.' Taking Physical Activity and Physical Education to School, Committee on Physical Activity and Physical Education in the School Environment, National Academies Press, 11/13/2013

Benjamin B. Wolman. 'Psychosomatic Disorders.' Springer Science & Business Media, 12/6/2012

Professor of Music Emeritus Lawrence Bennett. 'Breaking the Connection Between Emotional Pain and Physical Illness.' Dr. Lawrence Bennett, Masthof Press, 12/1/2008

Barbara Currie. 'The Illustrated Self-care Bible.' Maintaining Positive Self-care, Including Physical Health, Emotional Wellness, and Life-balance, Rachel Newcombe, Harper Collins Publishers, 1/1/2020

John F. Cryan. 'The Psychobiotic Revolution.' Mood, Food, and the New Science of the Gut-Brain Connection, Scott C. Anderson, National Geographic Books, 11/7/2017

Federico Bermudez-Rattoni. 'Neural Plasticity and Memory.' From Genes to Brain Imaging, CRC Press, 4/17/2007

Lynn Nadel. 'Cognitive Neuroscience of Emotion.' Richard D. Lane, Oxford University Press, 4/4/2002

Bennett Leventhal. 'Psychological and Biological Approaches To Emotion.' Nancy L. Stein, Psychology Press, 4/15/2013

James D. A. Parker. 'Emotional Intelligence in Education.' Integrating Research with Practice, Kateryna V. Keefer, Springer, 7/13/2018

Henry Dupont. 'Emotional Development, Theory and Applications.' A Neo-Piagetian Perspective, Bloomsbury Academic, 5/24/1994

Heather C. Lench. 'The Function of Emotions.' When and Why Emotions Help Us, Springer, 4/20/2018

Carroll E. Izard. 'The Psychology of Emotions.' Springer Science & Business Media, 10/31/1991

George Rosen. 'A History of Public Health.' JHU Press, 4/1/2015

Paul E. Griffiths. 'What Emotions Really Are.' The Problem of Psychological Categories, University of Chicago Press, 4/15/2008

Simo Knuuttila. 'Emotions in Ancient and Medieval Philosophy.' Oxford University Press, 1/1/2004

Clifford Whittingham Beers. 'The Mental Hygiene Movement.' Origin and Growth, Plimpton Press, 1/1/1917

Joanne M. Flood. 'Wiley Practitioner's Guide to GAAS 2022.' Covering All SASs, SSAEs, SSARSs, and Interpretations, John Wiley & Sons, 3/29/2022

Narayan Changder. 'MENTAL HEALTH.' Changder Outline, 3/12/2024

Osho. 'Emotional Wellness.' Transforming Fear, Anger, and Jealousy into Creative Energy, Harmony/Rodale, 4/3/2007

Adam Oakley. 'Undisturbed.' A Guide to Emotional Wellness, CreateSpace Independent Publishing Platform, 11/21/2014